Dedication

This book is dedicated to my wife Maureen and my sons Sean and Jaimie for their limitless patience while I was writing it, and to the teachers who contributed many of the solutions to behaviour problems. I would also like to express my thanks to Edna for bearing with me, and for typing the manuscript, often with very little notice.

D1635869

in the classroom

Practical Solutions for
Everyday Problems

David Wright

Heinemann Educational Publishers
Halley Court, Jordan Hill, Oxford OX2 8EJ
a Division of Reed Educational & Professional Publishing Ltd

OXFORD   MELBOURNE   AUCKLAND
JOHANNESBURG   BLANTYRE   GABORONE
IBADAN   PORTSMOUTH (NH) USA   CHICAGO

Heinemann is a registered trademark of Reed Educational &
Professional Publishing Ltd

02 01 00

10 9 8 7 6 5 4 3

British Library Cataloguing in Publication Data

ISBN 0 435 80855 9

Typeset by Techtype Ltd

Printed and bound in Great Britain by Biddles Ltd,
www.biddles.co.uk

CONTENTS

AUTHOR'S NOTE

This is a practical book for teachers and managers who want to improve their skills in behaviour management. The approach is based on the work already done by Bill Rogers, who I am indebted to for inspiring me to write this book. Academics should refer to his writing, *Behaviour Recovery. A Programme for Behaviourally Disordered Students in Mainstream Schools*, for the theoretical explanations underpinning the suggestions made in this book. If my work gets teachers talking about how they manage behaviour it will all have been worthwhile.

David Wright

INTRODUCTION

Children learn about the world in a variety of ways, and one of the most potent is through the examples adults give them. We model the behaviour and mannerisms that we want children to learn and from an early age they will emulate our habits and speech. Even their games are based upon adult occupations as they mimic the actions of doctors and nurses, and mothers and fathers.

Children learn about the values of society in the same way and notions of right and wrong become instilled and will often stay with them for life. Sometimes, however, contradictions occur which can be confusing. How often have you heard sayings like: 'you have to be cruel to be kind', or 'it is a war for peace'. You may even have found yourself shouting out 'be quiet!'.

Acting as a role model

Teaching is often based on modelling the desired behaviour and so it is important that we are clear and consistent in the way we do things. This goes beyond what we say and includes how we say it, after all if you want children to respect themselves and others you have to show them respect. Interrupting them when they are talking, and shouting orders at them will not be read as it is okay for teachers to shout but not students. They will adopt your ways. Equally if you do not want them to be violent, you should avoid using aggressive methods.

Learning new ways of behaving takes time and requires practice. You need to be patient and give the students the opportunity to learn and internalise the new ways, offering praise whenever they get it right.

The students will look to you to be fair and consistent. When you tell them to do something such as to look at you when you are talking, do not begin talking until all of them are paying attention. In this way you will reinforce what you are saying.

Offering and making choices

Life is about choices and being able to make the right ones is a useful skill. When a person chooses for themselves they are more likely to stick with what they have chosen. Offering choices as a means of managing behaviour, shifts the emphasis from compliance to co-operation. Instead of being told what to do, the students are deciding for themselves. The role of the teacher is in helping the student understand what options are available, and what the consequences will be for each choice, e.g.:

T Either hang your coat on the peg or accept that it may get trodden on and dirty.

This book provides strategies for resolving behavioural problems by offering choices and suggests ways for dealing with students who make the wrong choice or who refuse to choose.

The student is encouraged to develop their own self-image, and allowing them to be in control to make their own decisions is part of that. The focus is always on the behaviour itself and not the student. It is possible to modify behaviour more easily than trying to change attitudes.

A student who feels good about himself will be more open to the idea that he has made a mistake and it is only a temporary thing and can be put right. Students need to feel that we believe in them and are right behind them, helping and supporting them. Then they will trust us and make the effort. If they feel we have categorised them and relegated them to 'the land of no hope' they will give in as well. Behaviour recovery programmes are based on the belief that students are individuals capable of making choices and able to change the way they do things.

Developing strategies

Undesirable behaviour can be graded from the least obtrusive such as passing notes across the room and calling out instead of raising hands, to the most obtrusive which could include swearing, fighting and harassment. Teachers need to develop a repertoire of strategies in advance so they can deal with these kinds of incidents using a graduated response. The consequence should be in proportion to the action. It would be inappropriate for example, to give the whole class a detention because one student kept on chattering in the lesson.

Breaking the rules

It is important to focus on the primary behaviour that causes a rule to be broken. A student who goes walk about without permission breaks the rule of staying in his seat. Other incidents may have occurred while he was out of his seat but these are examples of secondary behaviour and should be put aside so that the primary behaviour can be dealt with. The student may try and justify the secondary behaviour and may even be in the right:

S   John tripped me deliberately so I thumped him! He asked for it.

But if he had not broken the rule, he would not have been tripped up. You can talk to John about what he did later.

Sometimes students exhibit secondary behaviour as a means of retaliation. Take the case of the girl who had been asked to remove her nose stud.

T   Jane, you know the rule on nose studs because you were told to take it out yesterday. I see you are wearing it again. Either remove it and give it to me, or your parents will be telephoned and asked to come to the school and discuss it.

S   Why should I?

T   Don't answer me back!

S   You can't stop me.

T   Would you like to find out?

S   You lay one hand on me and I'll sue you for assault. I know my rights.

The teacher began well but the student gave an arrogant reply which he did not like. Instead of ignoring it and leaving the student sitting outside the office, while he telephoned the parents, he rose to the bait and responded to the secondary behaviour which led straight to a conflict. It is better to remain dispassionate and calm and put all your efforts into dealing with the broken rule, not the behaviour that may develop as the student struggles to evade the consequence.

Why do students deliberately break rules and misbehave? It may be that they are trying to get attention and by behaving in an unacceptable way it will make the teacher angry and so evoke a response. If this is true, then the best thing to do is to remain calm and unruffled so as not to feed their need for attention. Firm but fair treatment focusing on the broken rule sends out the message that you are in control of your own emotions as well as the situation itself. When a punishment is necessary it should be given as a consequence of the behaviour not as a means of revenge. It should provide an opportunity for students to understand what they did wrong and reflect on how they will 'fix' it. The target is to get the students to own their behaviour and take responsibility for the consequences of it. This is only achieved when the students recognise what they did and are taking steps to put things right themselves.

Sometimes it is best to tactically ignore a student who has broken a rule, and reinforce the right kind of behaviour. Students who call out instead of raising their hands should not gain your attention. By ignoring them and taking the answer from someone who keeps the rule, you are demonstrating the behaviour you want. Eventually they will realise that the only way to get your attention is by doing as you ask.

Redirection

In certain cases, redirection of the student will gain a more positive response. Minor rule breaks like looking out of the window, turning round and chatting too much in the lesson are best dealt with by directing the student back onto the task:

T   This work should be done in silence Brian so turn round and get on with it please.

The teacher reminds the student of the rule and redirects him in a firm but friendly way back to what he should be doing. Redirection is less obtrusive and more likely to lead to a co-operative response from students who are not continually misbehaving. Obviously, repeated incidents in the lesson will require a graduated response to achieve compliance.

People respond to directions at different speeds so it is important to give a student some take-up time. Following redirection turn away and allow them time to respond rather than standing over them expectantly. The essence of good behaviour management is the same as teaching: how you say something (tone); what you say (content); and when you say it (timing). They determine how effective you will be.

In the push for improved standards in schools, effective class teaching is one of the most important catalysts for change. Good lessons can only take place if the teacher has control in the class. With good order, a teacher can try out and develop a repertoire of teaching styles.

School policy

All schools have rules to protect the rights of the individual. It is everyone's duty to observe the rules. This can be achieved by prescribing the behaviour required in a policy. The policy can cover many aspects of school life including: the uniform, school trips, use of school property and buildings. It embodies the ethos of the school and incorporates other policies like Equal Opportunities. Parents, governors, staff and students should be involved in its design and implementation to ensure it will be supported. This will encourage everyone to view it as an instrument for developing the school rather than something that is being imposed on them.

Once the school has formulated a behaviour policy training needs should be identified. New initiatives require new skills to make sure they can be implemented successfully. The staff must feel confident to deal with incidents that will arise because of the new policy. The training should offer strategies that are in line with the ethos articulated in the policy.

This book provides a range of scenarios and case studies to enable you to think about behaviour management and develop new skills that will avoid conflict and enhance co-operation between you and your students.

How to use this book

The scenarios and case studies are grouped in a way that will help you to develop your skills in these areas. As there is considerable overlap in the sorts of incidents the table below shows a number of common sources of conflict and where they can be found in the book.

Sources of conflict	Page number
Breaking rules	25, 47, 88, 89, 133, 136
Bullying	58, 61, 78, 81
Classroom drama	45, 63, 65, 66, 67, 68, 106, 110, 121, 123, 125, 127, 130, 131, 137
Fighting	56, 84, 91
Interruptions	1, 2, 5, 8, 11, 14, 16, 18, 27, 31, 32, 34, 37, 73, 97, 98, 100, 104, 106, 115, 118, 128
Swearing	51, 54, 55, 93
Vandalism	76, 87
Coming off task	22, 23, 29, 35, 41

1

THE NOISY CLASS

Introduction

The days of total silence in the classroom seem to have almost disappeared. The learning activities that students engage in are, in most cases, organised in such a way that discussion is an important feature and will enhance the understanding of the concept being taught. Discussions may range from the teacher addressing the whole class, to small groups working on a problem together. The framework of the discussions will be one of questioning and answering. For example, you may explain how a plant uses sunlight to produce nutrients, and then question students on the details to test their understanding. Alternatively, you may ask students to investigate something and they will try to identify the questions they need to ask in order to find out something new. In both these cases, the focus of the discussion will be the work that you have set. Successful outcomes will be achieved if the students understand what is expected of them and how they should behave.

When the discussion wanders you will need to be in control so that you can bring the students back onto the task quickly, quietly and authoritatively. The degree of control that you can exercise will depend upon a number of things. These will include:

- A clear agreement of how students should behave in the class.
- A respect for you and what you are trying to teach.
- Your willingness to assume the directorial role and exert your will when required.

A well organised class will exhibit these characteristics and provide a good learning environment. As students begin to divert their attention from the task, you will be able to bring them back from their gossip and chit-chat in a smooth, friendly but firm way.

The aim of this chapter is to present a range of strategies for some typical situations where talking becomes the barrier to learning. These strategies are not designed to eliminate noise totally from the class because that may be adverse to the mode of learning. If the students feel that the classroom atmosphere is oppressive they may not willingly want to enter into any discussion about the work, so the emphasis is on you having sufficient control to ensure your students are enthusiastic and remain on task, but do not obstruct others with the noise they make.

The key to an industrious class, where there is a buzz of student activity, properly focused and producing the desired outcomes is that everyone has a clear understanding of how to behave. The students and teacher need to know what is required and be aware of the rights and responsibilities of each person in the room. Tactical avoidance of disruptions in the class is your best strategy and the suggestions that follow will include some ideas on how to plan your lessons in ways that will minimise disruptions.

Talking during silent work

You have designed an activity that does not require the students to talk to each other at all. The only discussion that you may allow is if a student needs to clarify the instructions with you, otherwise, you expect them to work silently for an extended period of time. Midway through the activity several students begin to talk in low voices to each other.

Your strategy

Go over to the students and quietly remind them that the class is engaged in an activity that does not require any discussion, and that by talking they may be preventing others from concentrating. They may want to enter into a discussion about the work which could also disturb the rest of the class. If they do, remind them that it is silent work but you will be happy to help individual students with any difficulties they have. It is important to keep this kind of assistance to individuals as any wider discussions invite other students to involve themselves.

Your approach

The emphasis of your approach should be on getting students back on task which is best done in a firm, friendly way with a smile. Do not order students e.g. 'Stop talking!' or 'I said no talking.' Be polite, and also do it quietly by going over and speaking directly to them, otherwise your attempt to quieten them will actually break the silence and add to the problem.

T   This is silent work, raise your hand if you want to talk to me, thanks.

Resist the temptation to ask them what they are talking about. This is of no consequence as you have instructed the class that it is silent work and needs no discussion. When teachers do ask, the students take the opportunity to defend their position and usually reply that they were talking about an aspect of the work. You will be left in a weak position because you then have to try to explain that, although that may be seen as a good thing because it shows interest, it is not the behaviour you wanted. Furthermore, other students will over-hear and feel that the excuse was very plausible and you are being unreasonable. They may then enter the discussion or they may begin talking about your lack of 'firmness' to others in the class. Either way, the industrious silent atmosphere will have disappeared and be replaced with students off-task and feeling you are not really interested in them.

Redirection

It is important to be consistent, so if the problem recurs you should follow the same approach. Go to the students concerned and quietly redirect them back onto task by reminding them of the rule. Then move away as if you expect them to do as you ask. Allow take-up time for the message to sink in. If they continue, return and repeat your request but more firmly, again turning away to enable them to read the situation themselves.

Some teachers believe that standing over the students, staring at them will make them do what they want. Such an approach may get the students to do your bidding in the short term, but it is a confrontational approach and can appear quite threatening. The students will feel they have lost control over their own behaviour and the only choice they have is to do what you are asking.

The quality of the longer term relationship is at stake, and the students will probably show some reluctance to co-operate in the future in both the class and expected behaviour.

Establish ground rules

The most successful strategy to adopt is one that will minimise undesirable behaviour to begin with. You should discuss and agree with the class a code for the lessons, the first time you see them. Then remind them of the appropriate class rule at the beginning of each activity.

Arrangement of the classroom

This can be quite instrumental in ensuring that your lesson goes the way you want it to. One of the best ways of setting out the tables or desks for individual, silent work is in what could be described as a traditional layout. The desks are in rows running from the front to the back with spaces between each one. Ideally each student should have his or her own desk, but some schools have double desks so students will have to sit in pairs. The students will all be facing the front and if the room permits you could arrange the horizontal rows in lines like in an amphitheatre, so that every student is looking straight at you.

Chatting while the teacher is explaining something

You need to explain a concept or a process which requires you to talk to the whole class for an extended period of time. The exposition will be followed by some consolidation work where the class will apply the information you give them to a number of problems. Your talk will introduce new ideas and knowledge to the class, and you are expecting them to grasp the main points during it. They will be given some written information for the follow-up work but the emphasis will be on listening to you carefully. During this time some students begin chatting and making comments that cause the flow of your lesson to stop.

Your strategy

This is a common problem for many teachers. The chattering will have already broken the concentration of those involved and the students sitting near to them. The aim at this point is to minimise the disturbance and to get the whole class back on task which is to give you their full attention. Therefore your action should be one of not adding to the disruption, and more importantly, it should not cause any secondary behaviour that you will have to deal with. The best approach is to have in your mind a plan for dealing with these kind of interruptions that begin with the least obtrusive approach and moves progressively through a repertoire of strategies depending on the situation.

Your approach

During your exposition you should try to assume an authoritative air and have presence. Speak clearly and casually scan the room emphasising certain points to different groups of student. This will keep their attention. If students do begin to chat you should get their attention by looking straight at them. Direct eye contact is extremely effective so once you have it use a sign like holding one finger over your lips showing that you would like them to be quiet. As soon as the student gets the message, turn your attention away to another group of students and quickly resume your exposition. After a few seconds return to them and if the talking has stopped you can make another sign indicating to them that you have appreciated their response. Your stance and posture will communicate a lot to the class so during the lesson appear relaxed, open and animated. Smile frequently, especially when you need to redirect a student in the way described above.

Sometimes this approach will not be successful and the chatter may resume. If it is from a different student then the same method can be used, but if the same student begins talking again you may need to try a verbal approach. You will need to be more assertive to ensure your own right to teach is reinforced. Assertive behaviour need not be aggressive or threatening, simply decisive and confident, in a pleasant and friendly way. The tone of your voice will signal to the student that you are not angry but wish them to respond to your request because you are in charge of the situation. The kind of request you can make will be related to your right to teach and the right of the rest of the class to be taught. For example:

T   I am talking and I want you to listen, please.

This is a clear instruction directed at the individual student. You state what is happening in the class and what you expect the student to be doing. You put it politely and follow up with 'please' pausing momentarily, then turn your attention away with the expectation that he or she will follow your instructions.

Although you had to break the flow of your lesson the interruption is minimised and you can return immediately to it. As before, if your request is successful you should make known your gratitude to the student using a sign and a smile. There will be persistent chatter in most classes and so you may find yourself having to resort to these strategies quite often especially if the students are finding it difficult to stay interested.

Plan ahead

The best way of avoiding such situations is to plan in advance. Students will often have difficulty sitting passively for a long period of time when surrounded by their friends. The skill of the teacher is in holding the attention of the whole class by making the lesson sufficiently interesting. The information may be extremely 'dry' but in the hands of an enthusiastic teacher it can be brought alive. You need to regard your delivery of the lesson as a performance that will captivate, entertain and motivate your students to want to know more.

The length of the exposition will have a significant influence on the students. Most people's attention spans are limited, but they can be extended by change and variety (see Chapter 2 *Time wasters and off-task students*). Careful consideration of what you really need to deliver in a didactic way will help you to keep the exposition to an acceptable length.

Arrangement of the classroom

The arrangement of the room will also be a contributory factor in holding students' attention. You will want every student to have a clear view of you during the lesson. The seating needs to be organised to ensure this, which will also mean you will be able to have a clear view of the students. They should be facing you and not need to turn their head to see. Comfort plays a large part in this. Students who cannot see or hear clearly will fidget and eventually be distracted. Try to clear the room of unnecessary furniture and equipment and lay out the chairs allowing good access and individual space. Identify in advance a place for coats and bags, and open the windows to enable a movement of fresh air without freezing the students, or causing draughts that will rattle blinds and blow papers around.

Talking while students are presenting their work

You have arranged for the students to present their work to each other during the lesson. Each student will be required to stand at the front of the class and be given a set time period in which to explain their work. The other students will then ask questions for a further set time period. All students will be assessed for both their own presentation and their involvement in the presentations of the others. During one of the presentations several students begin to talk to each other which distracts the students presenting their work.

Your strategy

You can try the approaches suggested in the previous example first. Use non-verbal signs to indicate to the students that you want them to stop talking, remembering to engage in direct-eye contact and then look away as soon as they have got your message to allow take-up time. If they persist you will have to use verbal methods.

Your approach

Begin by gaining the attention of the student presenting and say politely:

T   Excuse me, Martin, could you pause for a moment please?

Then turn to the students who were talking. They will probably have stopped at this point and be waiting to see why you have intervened. You should engage their attention and give them an explicit direction.

T   Anisha and Jane, I would like you to stop talking please.

You do not need to appear angry, do it in an assertive and polite way. Be firm and direct and as soon as you have made this request, turn back to the student presenting, smile to put them at ease, apologize for the interruption and ask them to continue.

The use of positive directions such as, 'I want you to...' are less confrontational and let the students know what is required of them. They allow for a quick solution to take place so that the activity can be resumed. Negative statements such as, 'Don't talk while Martin is presenting', are best saved for situations which may be harmful when you need a quick response. In the example above they seem overbearing and are impersonal. They say nothing about your feelings and sound aggressive. Most students do not deliberately want to offend so they will accommodate your request. If you phrase your request as a question:

T   Would you like it if someone interrupted your presentation?

this simply invites a reply which will not resolve the problem. You have had to stop the presentation and now you will find yourself in a discussion with the student who caused the interruption. Your question will trigger secondary behaviour because it allows the student to make a comment on the work. A likely reply may be:

S   I wouldn't mind, it's a stupid lesson anyway.

Now how will you get out of that? The question has not clearly indicated what you want the student to do, nor has it resolved the interruption, instead it has sown a seed in the minds of some students that your activity may not be useful (even though it is). The situation has worsened to the point where you will have to skilfully redirect the whole class back onto the task which may not prove easy. So steer clear of questions in such situations and keep to direct requests.

Targeting your request by beginning with the name of the student, ensures they know you are talking to them. Always use first names and keep it friendly, after all it is only a small interruption and does not warrant a loss of temper or the use of stern or harsh attitudes. Save those for when they are really needed.

Plan ahead

You could minimise interruptions by planning. Give the students a task during the presentation such as formulating questions, noting the key points and preparing for the discussion. Brief them that their behaviour during the lesson is being observed and assessed, in particular their ability to listen attentively (a valued skill). If you have students who you know will be tempted to start talking or distracting others, give them a special task to do during the presentation part like being the official timekeeper. You will need to be clever in how you make this request. Explain that public speaking is a skill and needs to be succinct and not ramble so keeping to time is one of the most important aspects of it. Tell the class that you will need someone who can carry out the task accurately and fairly while still listening attentively to the speaker. You may get a number of volunteers depending on the age range, but you need to deliberate long enough to show that you have just made the decision of selecting your target student - possibly the troublesome one.

Run through the protocol for presentations before you begin. These will include turn-taking where only one person can talk at once and that will be the student doing the presentation. During the discussions use a signal like hands-up, for students wishing to speak. Stress to students that they should respect others and remain silent during the presentation as they will want to be treated in the same way.

Continuing to talk

If distracting behaviour occurs and the students do not respond to your request for quiet you will have to inform them of the consequences of their action. This may be that they will not be allowed to present their work, therefore they will not be assessed. If they have already presented then you can remind them that it is a two-way process and the assessment includes their ability to be a member of the audience and act appropriately.

Oral questioning with the whole class

You are teaching the whole class and every so often you check their understanding by asking them questions. However, a small number of students always seem to know the answer before the others and one or two call out the answer before you ask them to. This results in many students not attempting to answer and so you are not sure whether they have understood the work. How should you handle this situation?

Your strategy

This is a fairly common problem and it needs to be handled extremely sensitively. The students who are eager to answer your questions are keen and want to be noticed. They are looking for your attention and when allowed to give an answer will be hoping for your praise if they are correct. Such enthusiasm is valuable in a class and needs to be cultivated and maintained because it will be contagious and spread to the others if treated in the right way. It is important to let the rest of the students have a go at answering your questions as well, because although they may be slower to respond they may still be as keen as the ones calling out. Some students may be reluctant to speak out because they lack confidence and could be unsure of their answers. You will get to know your class and be aware of each student's ability. You will know which students are very able but do not like to show it, which ones have difficulty grasping the ideas and will not have an answer, and the students who are generally less confident about themselves. This knowledge of your class is invaluable and will help you bring out the best in each student.

The questioning of the class had a purpose in this scenario, it was to establish the general level of understanding. Therefore you do need to ensure that you achieve this by conducting the questioning in a way that brings in as many students as possible. The most obvious way is to direct your attention to a specific student by addressing him by name first, followed by the question:

T   Peter, can you tell me one thing that plants require to synthesise food?

Only Peter is being asked to respond and if he gives a satisfactory reply you can move on to the next question, directing it at another named student. In this way you can make sure that you find out specific things from each student which will give you an idea of their level of understanding.

Reminding about the rules

Other students will be tempted to give you the answer despite the fact that you have named someone else. If they call out before you invite them to speak you should ask them to signal that they want to contribute by raising a hand or using a similar sign.

T   It is nice to see you are keen, Michael, but it is not your turn. If you know the answer raise your hand and I will come to you.

You begin on a positive note, complimenting the student on his interest. You named him to avoid any confusion. You explained that turn-taking is being employed, and given clear instructions of what the student should do if he has the answer. You should not tell them off for interrupting by using 'don't' because it gives a negative signal to them which may cause bad feeling. What you are doing is expressing your pleasure in their enthusiasm while helping them to learn the right way to behave in the situation. When you ask a question and a student puts up his hand you go to him and begin by thanking him e.g.

T   Thank you, Michael, for raising your hand, I can see you would like to answer, go ahead.

This approach will reinforce the behaviour you are looking for and provide a positive feel to the lesson. If the student calls out again later in the lesson ignore him and move to someone with his hand raised and take his answer. You could begin with an acknowledgement that he observed the hands-up rule.

T   Iram, you have raised your hand, would you like to give us your answer please?

The other students are being reminded of the class rule in an unobtrusive and non-threatening way. They will also see that the right behaviour is rewarded as the student is allowed to give his answer. The subtle reminder of a rule until all the class have internalised it is the best approach.

Establishing ground rules

Preventative action will again be the most effective strategy. You should discuss how the class need to behave in this kind of learning activity at the start of the course. Get them to agree a set of class rules, then at the beginning of the lesson you can remind them of turn-taking and the hands-up rule. If a student does call out, you should remind them in a firm but polite way using positive 'do' instructions, in favour of negative 'don'ts'.

T   John, we have a class rule for calling out, please use it.

or:

T   Elaine, if you have the answer, raise your hand please.

You are naming the students to make sure they know who you are addressing and then you are clearly stating how they should act in this situation. A cheerful tone accompanied by a smile tells them you are not angry. You should not dwell on this but look from them to someone who has raised their hand and let them answer, showing them how it should be done and minimising the disruption. The movement of attention to another student prevents them from being embarrassed which may lead to a bad feeling that will cause secondary behaviour later in the lesson.

Excessive noise during group work

The class are engaged in project work in small groups. It involves some discussion so that the students can decide what is required and how they, as a group will tackle the work. After a while the discussions begin to get louder and students are raising their voices above a level normal for conversation. You feel that the level should be reduced. How do you achieve this?

Your strategy

The quickest and most obvious thing to do is to address the whole class in a voice loud enough to be heard by every student. They will be in groups so some students will probably have their backs turned and will not be able to see you, and if the noise level is loud in their group they will probably not hear you either if you speak normally. To be heard you would have to raise your voice to a point where you are shouting. In the meantime, the rest of the class will have stopped work and either be waiting for your next direction, or have lost momentum and have to get back on task, which will be a pity if they had been working well before you stopped them. So bellowing an instruction out will be relatively ineffective, as well as modelling the behaviour you are trying to alter. The message will be that raised voices are acceptable. Save this for when it is really needed such as an emergency or a situation that needs an immediate response like a fight between two students.

Your strategy needs to be completely effective and model the behaviour you want to see in the classroom at all times. The approach I suggest will take a little longer than a loud instruction directed at the whole class, but it will be more effective and can be adopted and used by the class for a variety of similar situations when you want their attention.

Go to the noisiest of the groups, and gain their attention by using a combination of eye contact, hand gestures and a simple request:

T   Will you all stop talking and look at me, please.

Excessive noise during group work

You can then either: explain that they are getting a little bit too loud and it is disturbing the rest of the class and preventing them from hearing each other; or you can tell them to conclude their discussion in two minutes and wait quietly for you to give new instructions to the whole class. You will give a signal that may be a visual one like folding your arms and facing the class expectantly. You may accompany it with a single word like 'okay'. When they see you do this they should stop, look, and listen immediately. You may want to combine your request for lowered voices and their attention so that you can get the whole class together again.

Then go round to the other groups as well and tell them that you would like them to stop and give your their attention when you give them the signal. Once every group knows what to do you are ready. Move to the centre of the front of the room, scan each group engaging the attention of one person in each group. Wait for a convenient time like a lull in the discussions and then give your signal. Make it clear and understandable. At the same time engage a student's attention in one of the groups furthest from you as these may not get the message as easily. Once everyone is giving you their attention you can proceed. If a group has not co-operated you will need to concentrate on these students a little more but resist calling out to them. Either direct your attention at them while maintaining your hold on the rest, or go over to them and quietly remind them that you have given your signal.

T Group B. I have given my signal please give me your attention, thank you.

Always smiling, and adopting a relaxed, open posture to show you are not annoyed but are waiting for them. Remember to praise the class for following your instructions:

T Well done, we will use that way of giving me your attention again, it worked very well.

The emphasis of this strategy is on your presence in the room and your friendly, but assertive attitude, indicating that you are leading the class and they need to be aware of your directions so that they will know what to do next.

Establishing ground rules

Before the activity starts you can brief the class on how they should conduct their discussions, using turn-taking and perhaps even nominating a chair person to keep order. This will provide a structure to the discussion and minimise the noise level. You can instruct them on what to do when they get your signal, and tell the class that you are relying on them to take responsibility for their behaviour, putting the emphasis on their self-control.

Managing group work to control the noise level is a skill and can be developed. Having good control will enable you to move around the groups and help them as well. Call them all back together when you need to.

Students not quietening down at the start of the lesson

You want to talk to the whole class together so you start to get their attention but a number of students continue to chat to each other. You stand waiting in expectation but they show no signs of stopping. Several other students try to be helpful by calling out 'Ssssh!' and 'Quiet!' which adds to the noise.

Your strategy

The class have got into bad habits and feel it is acceptable to enter a room and make a lot of noise. There are a number of ways of bringing the class to order and these involve you assuming control in an assertive way. The younger age groups will respond to an approach that involves repeating the start of a lesson until it is right. For example:

Students not quietening down at the start of the lesson

T   Right (said loudly, but not shouted) that was not a very good start. I expect you to file quietly into the room, sit down, take out your books and wait for me to call the register.

They may all stop talking at this point if they see you are cross and if so, you can remind them of the class code and then call the register, breaking off if they resume their chatter during it. Sometimes this method will have no effect and so you must try something else.

T   Okay. Everybody, outside the room and line up in an orderly way. We shall do it again.

Once outside, get them quiet and explain how you want them to behave. Tell them that if they do not get it right they can all come back and practise at lunchtime until they do. This will often do the trick but if you are not satisfied you could give them one more chance and then decide whether they should give up their lunch break.

It may only be a few of the students who are chatting, in which case you could ask them individually if they would like to be quiet so you can speak, or whether they would prefer to come back and practise entering the room in silence at lunchtime. Faced with a choice, they will probably go for the easy option and give you their attention.

Reminding about the rules

This method may seem very disruptive but it does make the point so that the class behave how you want them to. When you have them back in the room and seated you can call the register and then discuss the classroom code with them and agree on what kind of behaviour is acceptable.

Finally, a word about the students who were trying to help quieten the class. They are your allies, they want to help and so they need to be treated sensitively. For example:

S Ssssh!

T Thank you for your help, Aaron. Leave this to me (smile and be friendly).

Early into the lesson return to him and give him an opportunity to do or say something that will make him feel special or important.

Threatening to give the whole class a detention

You have had enough. The class do not seem to be responding, you have tried your best but they just persist with their chit-chat. Eventually you run out of patience and find yourself saying 'Anyone who talks will do a detention'. The moment you finish speaking a student sitting at the back mutters something.

Your strategy

This is one of those situations that teachers do not like to get into because the chances are that someone in the class will find it hard to conform and so be given a detention. It is also very hard for younger students to switch from an atmosphere of chatter to total silence. Why should they without some explanation? All they have to go on is your expression of displeasure, but because you have asked them to stop talking several times without any effect it appears that you do not really mean it. Finally, you have had enough, why should they believe you now? Of course some students will take notice but there will nearly always be one or two who will not. The boy in this example probably thought you would not hear him and anyway, he was prepared to risk being heard.

Sometimes things do not go according to plan and day-to-day difficulties that you would normally handle calmly escalate, so you need to find ways of cooling things down. In this example you will have to keep your word. Try to imagine what would happen if you lose your composure.

T Right Carl, I did warn you about talking; you will do a detention for that.

Threatening to give the whole class a detention

S But Sir, I didn't say anything!

T Yes you did, Carl, I heard you muttering to Alan, don't try to deny it.

S But Sir, I wasn't talking. I was just asking if I could borrow a pencil.

T I don't wish to argue with you. My decision is final, you'll do the detention and let that be a warning to the rest of you.

Now Carl feels he has been singled out and made an example of. He claims he was not talking but of course he was. He felt that asking to borrow something was different. The teacher is angry and not acting in a very rational way. The outcome is the student is being punished for something he feels he did not do. The rest of the class will feel the teacher has been unjust and side with Carl. The atmosphere in the class will be a difficult one and result in a poor climate for teaching and learning.

The teacher warned the students of the consequence if they continued to talk. Carl broke the rule and the teacher is obliged to follow it up but as you can see, he did not manage to calm things down in the way he would have liked. He got drawn into an argument in front of the whole class and they were the jury. Valuable time was wasted as he tried to re-assert himself. The whole thing got out of control as he over-serviced Carl's secondary behaviour. He should have postponed the actual consequence until later:

T Carl, I heard that. See me at the end of the lesson please.

S But Sir, I didn't say anything.

T Let's discuss it later, we have work to do now (said in a non-threatening but a 'I mean business' way).
Right everybody, turn to page 33 etc ...

S But Sir ... Sir ... I ... that's not fair.

Carl protests but the teacher tactically ignores him and continues with the lesson and does not over-service his pleadings. Eventually Carl goes into a silent sulk which enables the rest of the class to get back to work. The teacher can return to Carl and offer him help but if he continues to sulk and protest by refusing to work the teacher does not respond:

T   I am happy to help you with your work, Carl, so when you are ready raise your hand and I will come to you.

When the teacher sees him at the end of the lesson they discuss the problem more privately and calmly. Carl can explain why he was talking and the teacher can help him to understand that the class were told to be silent. Then he can begin to see he had been wrong to talk and together they can start to repair the relationship. He may still resent the detention and the teacher may feel that it is no longer appropriate. The class will have seen Carl being detained and feel he was being punished so it may not be necessary to go any further.

The incident was an unfortunate one and the teacher lost his self-control. Carl had not obeyed the instruction but equally, he felt he was not doing anything wrong. The chat after the lesson enabled them both to come to an agreement and allowed the teacher to let Carl off without compromising his position. When Carl tells his friends he has no detention it shows that the teacher can be reasonable (not weak).

Establishing ground rules

Why did this incident happen? The reason was that the teacher did not establish a clear code of behaviour in the class, which led to a gradual breakdown in his control of the lesson. A code helps everyone in the class know what is acceptable but students do need reminding at the start of lessons until they have got into the habit. Occasionally, someone forgets a rule and when it happens you should be able to remind them in an unobtrusive way. Teachers have good and bad lessons and sometimes things do not go according to plan. The important thing to do is get yourself back under control as quickly as possible so the students do not get confused about what is expected of them. We cannot be perfect all of the time, but we do need to recognise that we shall not be, and plan for it.

Summary

A class that generates noise is not necessarily a badly behaved one, it is not even a badly managed one. Discussions do need to be organised to avoid excessive volume and the students should be aware of when they should give you their full attention so that you can teach and give instructions. In this chapter I have offered a number of typical scenarios that all teachers will encounter at some point in their careers. Many of them are common to most lessons.

Key points for managing the noisy class

- Learning often requires discussion.
- Adopt an open, relaxed posture when addressing students.
- Smile and be polite when giving instructions.
- Use a firm, assertive tone when directing students.
- Address specific students by name and engage them with direct eye contact.
- Always allow a period of take-up time for your instruction to 'sink in'.
- Make positive 'do' directions, not negative 'don'ts'.
- Never get drawn into protracted discussions about what a student was doing. Clearly redirect them to what you want.
- Plan ahead, discuss class rules with the students and agree a code of behaviour.

2

Introduction

Sustaining the attention of thirty students long enough to complete a piece of work is the challenge teachers face daily. Younger students often have a shorter attention span than older ones. The skill lies in knowing your class and matching activities to the ability of every student. This is not easy because many classes have an extremely wide range of ability. The activity provides part of the solution, however successful teachers will often use a number of related activities in a lesson to create a series of new beginnings. As the newness of an activity wears off another activity is introduced which revives the student's interest. Thus, an hour lesson may have a minimum of three new beginnings. The rekindling of interest at the start of each new activity results in the overall average attention being greater than if there had only been one activity. The diagram illustrates how the student's attention is kept up by each new task. It will gradually fall, during the hour but much less than the single activity lesson.

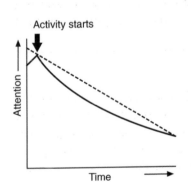

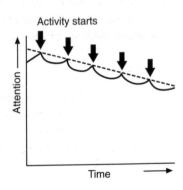

There will always be at least one student who cannot maintain attention for as long as the others. It is this student who will test your classroom management skills. Sometimes the content and pace of the lesson are not the cause of students losing concentration, other events happening outside may be distracting. Nevertheless you want to teach so you will need strategies that will help you do so.

This chapter deals with a variety of commonplace problems such as students turning up to the lesson unprepared; without homework; daydreaming; wandering around the room; and eating during the lesson. There are useful strategies for each situation to help you plan your own ways of dealing with these kinds of problems. Careful handling of each individual case is essential and asserting your authority in following up broken rules will be crucial in ensuring that students learn the right way to behave. The emphasis is on getting the students back to work as quickly and unobtrusively as possible.

Students not paying attention to a video programme

> The students have been asked to prepare a short presentation and you are showing a video programme to help them with their research. The video tape has been borrowed from a colleague who works in another school and she needs it back that evening. During the programme you notice a student staring out of the window. Bearing in mind that there will not be another chance to view the programme, what should you do?

Your strategy

The use of video programmes must be considered very carefully. If a class has not been taught how to use video material as a source of information, and if they do not find it entertaining, they stop watching and end up gaining nothing from it. The challenge is to engage the whole class and keep them watching so that they will benefit from the programme.

The problem of the student not paying attention can be avoided with the right planning in advance. Watching television for information purposes is a skill that can be developed just like reading for information. The difference between them arises from the way information is presented. With television, things pass very quickly and students need help in deciding what to extract and how to note it down. The first step is to give the students worksheets that signpost what you want them to look out for. This also gives them something to do so that they do not passively view the programme. Then, if anyone missed something he or she can obtain the information from another student. You may need to encourage and nurture this climate of sharing but it is a worthy virtue for the class to have.

You may not always want the class to make notes about the programme as it distracts them from viewing specific things like the actors' performances and the cinematic detail. For example, a reason for showing a televised version of one of Shakespeare's plays may be to help the students see how the lines on the page can be interpreted by the actors and come alive. In situations like this some students may lose concentration. They may fidget, look out of the window, doodle or even distract others by talking. This is where you will need to intervene to prevent the rest of the class getting sidetracked as well.

Redirection

You should try to help the student refocus his attention back onto the programme. Begin with the least obtrusive action. Walk slowly down the aisle to his desk and get his attention, then in a lowered voice suggest that he sits round and watches because he will have to discuss it with the others in the class. If this does not work you may have to repeat it so wait in the vicinity of his desk but do not make it appear as though you are standing over him. You can then return to him without interrupting the others.

You could stop the programme and ask questions about it in the hope that you can get him away from his day-dreams but this is obtrusive and will interrupt the rest of the class as well. You could also stand at the front and reprimand him but this will draw attention to him which will have a negative effect. Calling out above the soundtrack of the programme will mean you have to compete with it for attention.

Plan ahead

The best strategy is one of prevention; plan how you will use the programme and brief the students about how to view it. Make sure you tell them what you will want them to do afterwards.

Failing to hand in homework

During the collection of homework you notice one student sitting quietly without his book. When you ask him for his work he says that he was absent when it was set and did not know he had to do it. You check your register and discover that he was present.

Your strategy

When homework is set, a date is given for when it must be handed in and every student is expected to do it. Anyone who fails to complete the work without a good reason must be dealt with and the rest of the class need to know about it. Students who manage to meet the deadline will feel that it is unfair if someone is let off, and homework will lose its value and not be taken seriously.

Illness may be a reason for not getting the work done but it is not an exception. There are students and even some parents who think that if you are absent you do not need to make up the work. They need to be made aware that all the work is important and must be done, especially homework where the marks are recorded and used to reach a summative grade of the student's performance when reporting to parents.

On the day you set homework you could post the instructions home to absent students if you have the time. This is worth doing because it saves time in the long run as you do not have to repeat explanations and chase up pupils who missed it. You could place the instructions in their tray or locker if they have them or place named copies in your register for when they return. Planning in advance is the best way of minimising this problem.

Dishonesty

The issue of dishonesty arises when the student tries to escape the responsibility of making sure he completes his work on time. By lying he is showing you that he feels guilty. He may even believe that you will be deceived and he will get away with it. Before you try to resolve it, decide what you want to achieve. Do you simply want to get him to do the work so there is no gap in his learning? Will that satisfy the students who got their work in on time? They may feel that he has had more time and will get an undeservedly higher grade. A way round this is to have a system that assesses effort as well as the outcome. A very simple system that is easy to use awards grades of between A to E for the work produced and numerical grades between 1 to 5 are given for the effort and this is compatible with the GCSE grading. Sixth Form courses can be graded using the Key Skills criteria for the units for 'Improving Own Learning' and that underpins GNVQ and A Level pro-grammes. Students will come to relate their efforts to the grades they receive which is very motivating.

Once you have succeeded in getting the student to do the work you should discuss with him why he lied. Show him your register as proof that he was in the lesson when you set the work, then steer the discussion around to the reasons that prompted him to be dishonest. Help him understand that he is at risk of losing your trust by telling fibs, and that he will still have to do the work so dishonesty does not pay. Finish on a positive note by offering your help with the work and getting him to agree to come to see you if he cannot do it in future. Next time you see him outside the lesson make a point of being friendly and rebuild the relationship.

A disruptive student is disturbing the rest of the class

One student in your class is finding it hard to settle down and has got up and wandered around the room on a number of occasions. This is causing a disturbance and is beginning to lead to a breakdown in the behaviour of the others.

Your strategy

The secret to managing any movement in the room is in how you set up the class in the beginning. When the students have a set of ground rules they will know what they can and cannot do which will lead to an orderly environment where everyone can have the opportunity to learn.

Reminding about the rules

Younger students will probably need reminding of the rules quite often, and it is well worth emphasising the ones that they should follow for a particular lesson. The older students will pick up the routines quite quickly but they do forget at times so a reminder would not go amiss if you are doing something out of the ordinary. When the student starts to wander you can use the rule to get him back to his seat. For example, Michael was out of his place annoying one of the girls.

T   Michael (in a subdued voice and close enough not to distract the whole class). What are you doing?

S   Nothing, Sir.

T   I can see that (with a smile at Michael and tactically ignoring what he was actually doing). What should you be doing?

S   I was getting a pencil, mine keeps breaking.

T   What should you do if you need something?

S   Put my hand up, Sir, but you were busy and I wanted to get on with my work. (He is trying to hide his time-wasting and appear conscientious.)

T   What is the rule if I am busy with someone? (He is refocusing Michael's thoughts back onto the whole rule not just the bits that suit his story.)

S   Wait quietly until you can come to me. (He says it in a sarcastic tone and folds his arms in a smart alec way.)

T   Good (ignoring the body language and tone of voice), so I expect you to use the rule next time.

The teacher finishes with a smile and an offer of help that shows that the matter is ended and there is no bad feeling. He gets the student to do what he wants by cleverly questioning him rather than issuing orders. When he asked Michael what he was doing he was allowing him to give an explanation. After all he may have had a reasonable excuse. Many children will reply with 'nothing' when asked what they are doing because they are aware that they are doing something wrong. The teacher agrees with Michael because he should be doing his work. Michael feels pressurised so he makes up an excuse about the pencil. This opens up the way for the teacher to help him learn and use the rule properly. He does not get involved in arguing about what Michael was really doing – annoying the girls. Instead, he asks him what he should do when he needs something. (The rule reminder). This helps Michael see where he went wrong and tell the teacher what he is supposed to do.

Throughout, the teacher has refrained from telling the student what to do in order that he will think for himself. Only at the end, does the teacher become assertive by stating what he expects. He does not give orders or pay obvious attention to Michael's body posturing, the mocking tone of his voice and his lies. He addresses the broken rule and ignores the secondary behaviour so that a resolution is reached.

Similarly, you should keep your sights on helping the student understand where he or she went wrong and how you want him or her to behave in the future. This may not always be possible at the time but certainly it must be done later. The name calling and arrogant behaviour is best dealt with as a separate issue.

Avoid conflict

The knack of dealing with these kinds of situations is to keep them fairly discrete and not turn them into public conflicts. I have seen many teachers deal with this type of problem by shouting across the room.

T   Colin! Where do you think you're going? (No time is allowed for a response as one is not expected.) Get back to your seat now or you'll be sorry. (A threat of a punishment closes the matter.)

S   But Sir, I was ...

T   Don't argue, just sit down and get on with your work.

The student goes back to his seat muttering under his breath. The matter is closed as far as the teacher is concerned but the boy feels he has been treated in an undignified way in front of the whole class. He may be resentful of this. Shouting across the room will disturb the other students and reinforces the use of noise; if the teacher raises his voice then the class will believe it is alright. There is no reference to the broken rule and no opportunity to rebuild the relationship, unlike the earlier case where Michael was helped and it ended with a smile.

The end-of-term party

One day near the end of the term your students approach you during a lesson and ask if they can have a party in the classroom. This will involve considerable organisation, responsible behaviour and gaining permission from the Headteacher so you feel you need time to think about it. How can you get them back to the work they should be doing without deflating their enthusiasm or raising their hopes?

Your strategy

Marking the seasons, festivals and milestones in the year is an important part of school life. Harvest festivals, prize-givings and the Christmas dances mark the passage of time and punctuate the rhythms of school life. School is not just about lessons, homework and examinations, it should also offer valuable opportunities to learn about the world beyond the textbook. One way this can be done is by allowing students to take responsibility for organizing an event. The class party is ideal because it is a small low-key event where students can experience a variety of jobs in a supervised environment. It will of course generate extra work for you so the decision to go ahead should not be taken lightly. That is why it is important not to respond immediately in order that you can think through all the implications and weigh them up. Explaining that you would like time to consider their request needs tact so they do not get the wrong end of the stick and think you are fobbing them off.

Your approach

The students should not have asked you about this until the end of the lesson but they often do not think and tend to have their own agendas. You can use their impulsiveness as a means of getting them started on their work again.

T   Well, that seems like it might be fun, but you are supposed to be writing up this experiment at the moment. If you go back to your desks and work extra hard for the rest of the lesson I shall think about your idea tonight and let you know tomorrow.

The teacher begins by complimenting the students on their idea, then reminds them of what they should be doing, demonstrating that their request is an interruption to it. Then the teacher can do two things: he can use the interruption as a bargaining tool and also defer making the decision.

Telling students that you will think about it later, is not necessarily agreeing to it. It is promising them that you will give it further consideration, but only if they work hard and earn that reward. If they really want it they will probably do as you say, then at the end of the lesson you can tell them that they had worked well and so you will think about their idea. This will give them a sense of victory and it will have served your purpose.

You will have to be careful when you tell them you will think about their request. Try to strike the balance between saying it sounds good and being assertive to get them back to work. If you succeed you will still have to decide whether you are going to allow them to have a party, but that is another issue.

Note passing during the lesson

> Turning to write on the board you are aware of a quick rustle of movement between several students. You do not respond and keep on writing, but out of the corner of your eye you see one student pass a note across the aisle to another. They do not think you have seen them.

Your strategy

The scene is almost comical and could be from an old episode of the popular television series of the 1960s, 'Please Sir'. However, things like this do actually happen and it is quite amusing to see what children use the note system for. The subculture of the classroom is communicated through this medium. Love affairs, after-school activities, jokes, ridiculous thoughts, vendettas and observations about the teacher all feature in their notes.

The important thing to remember when dealing with this is that the action you take should not disturb the flow of the lesson for too long. Home in on the students concerned if you know who they are, but if you do not you should wait until you are sure. Then at a convenient moment, when you can leave the front of the class, walk slowly to the students who were passing the note and address them together:

T   If the note comes back this way put it away, unless you want me to know all your secrets!

Smile and wink at them then move back to the front. Make the comment loud enough for the others nearby to hear. They will know you know about their note, but you are not turning it into an issue. The use of humour and sign language shows them that you are not angry but you want their note passing to stop. The choice remains with them so that they can own the decision. When you address several students and not one in particular you are allowing the real culprits to eavesdrop. Then, by turning away you are giving them all time to think and decide what they will do.

Redirection

On the occasions when you catch the culprit red-handed you should have a suitable comment at the ready to redirect them back to the work they should be doing. Humour helps here because it shows you want something done but are not trying to throw your weight around. For example:

T   Love letters are treasured items, I know I have a few! If you want to keep that one put it away and get on with your work. If you can't get on while you have it, put it on my desk - I'll read it later (wink and smile).

The letter may not have any romantic references but it does allow you to inject a little humour. It is not worth making a big thing out of because it is only a note. Offering the choice will probably lead to the student putting it away if the note is embarrassing. Throughout the incident you should be friendly and non-threatening so that you can get all those concerned back to work as promptly as possible.

Eating in lessons

During a lesson you are covering for a colleague you notice a student reach down to his bag, take out a sweet, unwrap it and start to eat it. The school rule clearly states that food and drink must be consumed during breaks and lunchtime only.

Your strategy

The immediate reaction of many teachers would probably be to reprimand the student there and then. The best approach is to first find out why the student broke the rule in order to understand his actions. Be friendly, smile and ask him whether he is aware of the rule about eating during lessons.

Reminding about the rules

If he says he is not aware of the rule, or had forgotten, you need to point out where and when eating sweets is permitted. He may be quite cocky and put on the innocent act, but you should not respond because you are reminding him of the rule so that he has had a warning. Next time you will regard it as a broken rule and act accordingly.

Alternatively, he may be quite upset that he did not know the rule and unwittingly broke it, so being sensitive to his feelings and talking it over with him is kinder than standing over him in a threatening way. Finish it with a few reassuring words and a smile and get him back to work. Return to him after a few minutes to check he is alright.

You may feel that he had not forgotten and had deliberately broken the rule. In which case you adopt a different approach by going straight to the rule-reminder. Point out that he has broken the rule and ask him what he is going to do about it. This places the responsibility with him and he will probably agree to keep the rule in future. You do need to follow this up with a reminder of the consequence for breaking the rule in the future. Remember, match the consequence to the broken rule. Finish by offering the student the choice so that he feels in control. The feeling of being powerless is very frustrating and leads to deeper feelings of resentment.

The emphasis is on finding out why the student broke the rule and remaining friendly throughout. The right approach will enable you to remain in control as well.

Forgetting to bring the right things to the lesson

For homework you asked the students to bring in some household items because you have planned something special for them. You checked that they all wrote it in their homework books. Then, while you are getting things ready at the start of the lesson a student comes over and tells you she has forgotten to bring her things in. The rest of the class are sitting patiently waiting for you to start.

Your strategy

This is something that most teachers will encounter. Even the best intentioned child is prone to forgetfulness. The burden of ensuring that children, especially the younger ones, do their homework, have the right kit for PE, dinner money, donations for fairs, etc often rests with the parents. What we are trying to do in partnership with the parents, is help each child take responsibility for preparing themselves for school. This takes time and needs to be taught.

When students forget something that they have been asked to bring in you need to have a contingency to ensure that they do not miss out on what you have planned for them. Have some spare sets of the resources you have asked the students to bring in.

Your approach

You need to find ways of preventing the students forgetting their things. You could send a letter home to the parents in advance. The timing of this is critical. If they receive it too early they may forget, and if it is too late they might not have time to prepare. A week's notice is about right.

You could arrange for everything you require to be brought in a week before the lesson so you know the resources are ready. This also gives you the week to chase up any forgetful ones and decide whether you need to provide resources yourself, so send the letter home two weeks before you need things.

Helping students remember

You do need to help the students remember things of importance. This can be done by giving them some strategies. Get them to note down things, because the act of writing them down will help commit them to memory. Younger students may need to be monitored to make sure they get the details right. This could be backed up with a note home informing parents of what you are doing and what will be needed. You may even ask parents to check that their child has done what they noted down in class. This approach is preferable to the parent doing it all because it encourages the student to be more self-reliant. After your deadline, you will be able to identify students who have forgotten and do something about it with time still to spare.

Some schools give every student a home-school contact book for noting down homework details. Parents may be asked to comment in it as well. This book is useful because parents can see what their child is being asked to do and the act of signing it confirms they have read it.

When a student is continually forgetful they may need very specific help and the strategies suggested here may require further development to fit your own needs. The main thing to remember is that a student who forgets and comes unprepared is increasing the demands put on you. The lesson is not the best time to sort out these problems, so pre-empting them will allow you to become more effective in solving them.

Protesting about a test

Nearing the end of a topic you decide to set the class a short test to find out how much they have learned. When you announce it there are painful groans and several students start to complain that you have not given them time to revise. How do you settle them down and get on with the test?

Your strategy

We do not like being judged by others, especially if we are unprepared as it makes us feel powerless and subject to the controlling influences of others. When students are tested they want to do their best and they feel that surprise examinations do not allow them to.

The surprise test causes behaviour problems which the teacher has to manage. On one occasion, a teacher begin her lesson as follows:

T   Right, good morning class, take out a pencil and clear your desks of everything else because we are going to do a short test.

S1   Oh Miss! ... etc.

S2   Come on, Miss, we haven't done any revision.

S3   Miss, that's not fair, you never told us.

S4   Well I don't know it so I'm going to fail anyway! (She turned away and reached to close her bag as a symbolic gesture.)

T   Quiet please ...(extended pause while the class slowly come to order). It will only take 20 minutes then you can continue with your projects. (This is an effort to appease the class.)

S1   But Miss, if I'd known I would have revised.

The teacher is in danger of getting involved in minor disputes. She needs to press on, but by ignoring their comments she will appear overly authoritarian. A number of the students have already resigned themselves to failing and are getting quite angry about the position they are in. The net result is a class who are unhappy and feel they have been disempowered. Furthermore, the teacher's position is being challenged. So how can you incorporate your students' needs with your own?

Giving an early warning of what you are going to do will help. Tell the class at the start that you will be testing them at the end of the topic. Offer them advice on how to prepare for the test, such as checking that they understand the work in each lesson, and to see you if they have any problems. Get students to read through their notes and rewrite them where necessary to ensure they are legible and make sense. Explain to the class why you are testing them, and make it clear that it will help you assess how much each student has learned and understood rather than what they can commit to memory in the short term. Then on the day of the test they will all know what is happening and have had a chance to prepare in a way that will enable you to gauge the knowledge more accurately. Any protests about revision can be answered by reminding them that if they have followed your advice from the beginning they will not need to worry about memorising things at the last minute.

This strategy will help alleviate any difficulties and get the class down to the test. You may still have one or two who are angry, but they will probably be more cross with themselves for ignoring your advice than cross with you. The responsibility of preparing will be with the student rather than with you, and so the surprise element will be minimised.

Calling out in class

The class are nearing the end of an assignment and have begun writing up their own conclusions. They are all working well except for one boy who is resting his head on the desk and you can see from where you are sitting that he has not written anything. Suddenly he sits up and starts calling across the room disturbing other students and distracting one boy in particular.

Your strategy

Children stop working for many reasons and you may not have the time to find out why during your lesson so you need to plan ahead, and also establish at the start what you expect them all to complete by the end of the lesson. The target is for every student to do the work successfully. You will need rewards and consequences to encourage students to make up work. Consistency is the key and once the class know you mean what you say they will begin to comply with your requests.

Your approach 1

This longer term approach allows you to deal with the more immediate problems like the one described. Behaviour like this can be quite common in mixed ability classes. In any year group you may encounter one or two children who seem to behave outside of the expected norms. They may be in the statement process or they may just be resisting for their own reasons. (See *Learning to Labour* by Paul Willis for a more detailed study of the social reasons for resistance). Whatever the reason, it is your job to teach all the students in the class so you need to find ways for dealing with this kind of disruptive, antisocial behaviour.

Reminding about the rules

The use of the established code and consequences is the most reliable strategy. For example:

T You have not written anything yet, can I help you?
(The student may say yes and you have lift-off! But he may decline your offer.)

S This is boring (he slouches, pouts and fiddles with his ruler). I can already do this, can't we do ... ? (He suggests something unrelated.)

T (Ignoring his secondary behaviour.) You may find it boring, but this is the work we are doing today. Would you like some help? (The teacher refocuses the student back onto the work by cleverly agreeing with him.)

S I'm not doing it, it's stupid, why should I? (He slouches further into the chair and starts to unzip his bag.)

T Well Andrew, the reason you should do it now is that if you need help I am available. If you don't do it then you will have to do it for homework. You know the rule 'all work must be completed' even if you are absent. (The teacher reminds Andrew of the rule.) Now let's see you begin it. (The teacher does not offer to help but turns away expecting Andrew to start work. When he does the teacher returns occasionally to check he is all right and offer help. But the student may refuse to get going.)

T   I see you still haven't started.

S   I told you, it's boring and I'm not wasting time on it. (He goes into a sulk, crosses his arms and looks away.)

T   Andrew ... Andrew, look at me please ... I am waiting. (He waits till Andrew looks up then speaks.) It is your choice, if you don't do it now you will have to do it later. I am expecting it to be complete by the next lesson, but if you don't you will have to face the consequences. (The teacher explains what these are.) Now decide please. (He smiles but uses an assertive tone to show he means it. Then he walks away to allow Andrew time.)

S   This is so boring.

Choosing the consequences

Andrew turned round and began his work but insisted on getting the last word by muttering about the work being too easy and dull. The teacher ignored his closing protests because he was getting down to work. If the student decides not to work, then he is choosing the consequence. You will have to ensure that he does not disturb the others, but if he does he can be moved or even asked to go to another place in the school where he will be supervised for the rest of the lesson.

The teacher used clear, short phrases that directed Andrew back to his work and made him aware of the consequences if he did not comply. He avoided the comments about the work being boring and did not respond to Andrew's negative behaviour. When it came to the showdown, the teacher first made sure that Andrew was looking at him and paying attention before he reminded him of the consequences of not completing the work. The matter of calling out was not mentioned because the teacher wanted to deal with one thing at a time. Children are not very good at responding to a number of requests made at once. It tends to confuse them and so the best line is to get them to understand, learn and perform one thing before moving to the next.

When you experience behaviour like Andrew's you may feel frustrated if students do not seem to respond to your request. Do not over-service their attention seeking, let them have some time alone to decide what they want to do. If they decide not to do the work they are deferring the consequence till later. You can let a student sit and not do any work if that is what they decide, but you cannot allow them to call across the room and disturb others. In Andrew's case, the teacher had let earlier incidents of calling out go and when he spoke to him it was about the work.

Your approach 2

You may prefer to challenge the calling out the moment it happens. The teacher in the following example had a well established classroom code and when a boy called out he moved in swiftly to talk to him.

T   Chris, you know the rule about calling out.

S   Yes Sir, but I was only asking Atif for a ruler.

T   Maybe you were, but what should you do when you want something? (He gets Chris to think about what he had done wrong.)

S   ... (silence) ... Dunno.

T   I am sure you do know, Chris.

S   ... raise my hand and wait in silence.

T   Good, so please use the rule in future. Now, do you need any help?

If he does need help you can give it and start to rebuild the relationship. If the same student starts to call out again later in the lesson, remind him that he had shown he knew the rule earlier during your little chat with him and that he has just broken it again. You should always follow a rule reminder with some kind of action to show you mean the rule to be kept.

Your approach 3

There are students who will not respond to the above approaches. They need a more individualised, structured approach which will enable them to see the extent of the problem.

Arrange to meet with the student and explain that uncontrolled calling out is disruptive and will prevent other people from learning. Give the student a pre-prepared sheet with 2 x 2cm squares on it. Get him to write the date of the lesson above a square. Then agree a visual sign with him that you will make whenever he calls out or misbehaves. His job is to put a mark in a square each time you make the sign. At the end of the first lesson see him and total up the marks then set a target for the next lesson that is achievable. For example, he may have fifteen marks, so you could try for twelve. Once he achieves the target reward his effort and set another one.

This method will help him realise when he is behaving in an unacceptable way and empower him to try to improve. Plenty of praise and small rewards will keep him going and small achievable targets will ensure he can be successful.

Asking to go to the toilet during the lesson

Midway through a lesson one of the girls in your class asks if she can go to the toilet. She has a reputation for skiving and is beginning to fall behind with her work.

Your strategy

Children of all ages may try to get out of lessons at one time or another. They will have many different reasons and they will not all be due to a dislike of the subject. Going to the toilet is a means of escaping and having a five minute break. It is reasonable to ask students to visit the toilet before coming to your class. Lessons are around one hour in length in schools, and double periods are two hours. Most children can hang on for an hour or two if they have been prior to the start, so the best solution is prevention. Tell the class what you expect and make sure they know it is their responsibility to visit the toilet as permission will not be given to go during the lesson. There may, of course, be exceptions because some children could have medical conditions and be unable to wait. You should be made aware of these cases, but if you are not it is worth finding out whether any of the class have any special medical needs.

Your approach

When a student approaches you to ask for permission to go to the toilet you will have to use your own judgement and, at the end of the day it will have to be one based upon trust. It is hard to stick rigidly to your guns when a child repeatedly asks to be excused because she genuinely wants to go. If you deny her request you may have to deal with a formal complaint from her parents.

The first time a child asks you, you could try your method out. Explain that she must try and hold on to the end of the lesson, but if she insists let her go and monitor her requests in the future. Speak to other teachers and find out if they have been asked as well. Some schools operate a system for students needing to leave the classroom. They have a space at the back of the homework books where the teacher records the date, time, room and reason for leaving, together with an estimated time of return. The student takes it with her and if she is challenged by staff or prefects she may be asked to show her books to verify her explanation. This is a very good way of preventing students from being wrongly blamed for wandering. Furthermore, it results in a record that tutors can use to pick up any trends or unusual behaviour. You could stress the need to complete the work in the lesson, otherwise it must be done at home. This would mean that the girl in our example is the only one with homework. She may think twice about going then. The consequence of not doing the work now is that it must be done later. If she chooses to go, you need to follow it up the next day to show you mean what you say.

Summary

Sustaining the concentration of the students is the key to good teaching. If they find the work interesting or develop a good work ethic they will gain a great deal, and those who fail to maintain their concentration will disturb the others and cause problems for the teachers. The solution lies in ensuring lessons are carefully planned and have achievable outcomes that are challenging and engaging. The teacher needs to have strategies ready for when students temporarily stray from the task. In this chapter I have worked through some typical scenarios that all teachers will encounter at some point, especially if they have a class with a wide ability range.

Key points for managing students who go off-task

- Establish a code of behaviour with all the groups you take, even the classes you cover.
- When one student goes off-task try to use unobtrusive methods so as not to disturb the rest.
- Ensure everyone, including those absent have details of the homework and know the deadline.
- Remind students of the rules governing movement in the class at the start of a lesson when you want them to stay seated.
- When students make requests that are unrelated to the lesson agree to consider them later.
- Obtain background information about the students before the first lesson.
- Have a contingency plan for the provision of resources that you ask students to bring in.
- Prepare students for tests by giving them plenty of warning of when they will be.
- Deal with attention seeking students away from the rest of the class.
- Offer students choices so they can own decisions about their behaviour.

Time wasters and off-task students

- When students go off-task get them to focus on the classroom code or the school rules to help them back to work.
- Plan ahead and develop strategies to help you deal with students who go off-task.
- Insist all students visit the toilet prior to your lesson because they will not be given leave during it.

3

Introduction

Considering the size of schools and colleges, it is hardly surprising that there are frequently conflicts between students, and between staff and students. The school 'community' is not a naturally forming one. Teachers and students do not come together voluntarily. Children under the age of sixteen must go to school by law, and teachers may work in any school where they can obtain a post but they do need to work to support themselves. Recognising this is a useful starting point and can help determine the style of behaviour management we choose to adopt. Some teachers go for the dominating, overtly authoritarian approach based on the assumption that whatever they say will be done and rule-breakers must follow their orders. There is no subtlety in their style and when they are crossed, a conflict ensues. The winners are the ones who can impose their will in open combat. Invariably the teacher wins but at what price?

The students must learn to comply under this regime but that does not mean they will co-operate. The teachers using this kind of discipline will probably survive and get through their careers relatively unscathed, but they must be strong, thick-skinned and be prepared for outright defiance every once in a while. They may also find that their tactics will lead to teacher-student relationships based on fear and hatred. The students will be uneasy and the teachers will not get as much from them. The inevitable outcome will be underperformance because there is no willingness to develop a two-way relationship where the students can blossom and reach their potential.

Avoiding conflict

The alternative approach is based on strategies that avoid conflict by removing the barriers preventing co-operation. For example, if a parent is in a hurry in the morning and needs to get the breakfast

45

ready for his children he should not ask them what they would like because they will want to look in the cupboard, then spend ages deciding and then changing their minds. Neither does he tell them they must have Rice Krispies because they will argue that they want something else. What he should do is offer them a limited choice.

'What cereals do you want for breakfast: Rice Krispies or Weetabix?'

Then, if they procrastinate he hurries them up by asking them to decide so they can own their choice. A choice of two is about right for little children, any more and they cannot cope. They invariably decide fairly quickly without an argument, but not always. If you can get it right 80 per cent of the time you are doing well as a parent or a teacher.

The same goes for students, they do not like to feel trapped, they want a way out that they have control over. Conflicts are avoided by looking for ways for your rule-breakers to climb down without losing face. Getting your way is the main objective but you do not need to rub the student's face in it. The secret is to be subtle and sophisticated, draw on your knowledge of how children behave that you gained during your training.

Dramas

The dramas that occur are often caused because of unavoidable accidents. A child is sick, a student has a fit, a boy gets a nosebleed. These are the kinds of things that happen in schools and they must be dealt with efficiently to avoid too much disruption. Whenever a drama occurs, children will become inquisitive and want to find out what is happening. It is not surprising really because we spend a lot of time and effort encouraging them to ask questions and investigate their world so that they will learn about it. Sometimes we need them to 'mind their own business' in a polite way because their attention becomes a source of embarrassment and makes the child at the centre of the drama feel awkward. At other times we need them to curb their inquisitiveness for their own good. The sight of blood or a child fitting can be extremely disturbing to the young, so they need to be shielded from unnecessary exposure to it. A teacher's skill is measured by how they can deal with the disruption to the lesson so that the class can return to their work.

It is amazing that there are so few incidents of this kind in schools considering the numbers of students. This is an indication of the co-operative adherence to the codes of behaviour expected in such a large group. Children quickly become socialised and understand what they can and cannot do. Some do not learn as quickly as others and some resist the system which is why problems occur.

Dealing with conflicts and dramas

This chapter highlights some of the more common conflicts and dramas such as: incorrect uniform, swearing, fighting, bullying, sickness and copying. There are explanations of how best to approach the perpetrators and victims, and useful strategies for dealing with each situation to help you think out your own approach in advance. Perceptive handling of each individual situation is the answer. Think ahead, agree with your colleagues some common strategies and remain consistent and fair at all times. Some of the examples in this chapter are commonplace but seem extremely difficult to deal with. Many teachers have sometimes turned a blind eye to them rather than get involved. Serious or tricky situations that affect others must be dealt with. Ignoring conflict situations is tantamount to condoning them and as teachers we owe it to all children: otherwise *Lord of the Flies* could seem like reality for some students.

Wearing incorrect school uniform

A student arrives at school wearing inappropriate clothing that contradicts the school dress code. This problem is becoming more widespread and parents are beginning to complain. They do not see why their children should be dressed correctly if others are not. You are on duty at the entrance and some parents are watching to see what you will do.

Your strategy

Schools where uniforms are worn stipulate what is acceptable and where the uniform can be purchased. Students arriving without an item of uniform may be loaned it for the day to ensure the uniform rule is upheld. This is relatively easy for ties, hats and even blazers but other clothing is more problematic. Jewellery and make-up can be dealt with on the spot by drawing the student's attention to the rule and instructing them to remove it. The main problem with a uniform is how it is worn e.g. the skirt is too short, the shirt is untucked, the tie is knotted in the wrong place. These are signs of students resisting the uniform. The students will argue that they *are* wearing the uniform unless clear guidance is given on how to wear it properly. Most students will respond to a direct instruction:

T   Tuck your shirt in before you go into school please, Steve.

Some students may pretend to do what you ask, for example Steve may pull up his shirt and hold it tightly to make it look like it is tucked in. When this happens, call them back and ask them to do it properly.

Students often do not see any advantage in wearing a uniform. They see it as something they have to do as part of going to school. Those who resist school may defiantly resist the uniform and others will copy them in an effort to fit in with the crowd. You will need to be more assertive and wily with them. They are testing the system to see what they can get away with. Firm action will normally work but you may find that several reminders are necessary before the message sinks home. The way you deal with this kind of student will determine whether you get a long-term solution or just a temporary one that will break down later.

Situation 1

In the following case, the teacher began well but then the student started to get the better of her.

Wearing incorrect school uniform

T   Alan, we have a rule about ear-rings. What is it? (She gets him to think about the rule.)

S   Dunno Miss. (He smirks cockily).

T   Only studs may be worn. Please remove the ear-ring and give it to me. I will put in the safe until home time.

S   I've only just had it pierced, and I can't take it out yet.

T   That may be true. (She agrees with him.) But the rule is studs only, so take it out please.

S   I can't ...

He starts to walk away and smiles at his friends who are watching. There is a buzz of excitement as he is acknowledged as the 'winner'. They admire his bravado and his reputation as a 'tough nut' is enhanced. Further action is required.

T   Alan! (He ignores her.) Alan, come here now! (Her expression is serious, her voice is loud and assertive and shows she means business.) I want those ear-rings out now.

S   Sorry Miss, I have to see Mr ... (he starts to walk off).

T   Alan, come here immediately, or you will get a detention!

Ultimately, she will win the power struggle, but at what price? The parents will have witnessed her losing her temper. Alan is the real winner in the eyes of the other students and he has got the attention he wanted.

There is a reason behind most disruptive behaviour. The student has a goal of his own, and Alan's was to gain admiration from his peer group. The subverted uniform is a sign of solidarity and Alan is expressing his affinity with the students and against the authority that imposes the rules. His challenge is made on behalf of his peer group and signifies one of the many struggles for control. We need to spot these bids for power, recognise why they occur and develop strategies that successfully deal with them.

Avoid conflict

It begins by staying calm and in control of our emotions. Every word, gesture and expression the student makes is designed to aggravate and needs to be read in that way. We need to conceal our anger and frustration and project an image of fairness and be friendly. You should resist making comments that show your frustration. For example:

T	I hope you don't do that at home.
S	(This is school and a different game).
T	Dear me, when will you ever learn?
S	(I'm not trying to learn your ways).
T	I am losing my patience with you.
S	(Good, I am starting to win this one).
T	If you did that in front of your parents, they wouldn't like it.
S	(You are not my parents and only one of us can win).

This will only succeed in fuelling the student's search for attention. By drawing attention to her in this way you will be showing that her actions are working and she is getting public recognition for resisting the established authority. This will increase her sense of belonging to the sub-group and strengthen her bid for power.

The best action is to shift the discussions to somewhere more private away from her peers and to avoid a public display of personal emotion.

Your strategy should not be to control, but be based upon adherence to the school rules. Identify the student's goal for resisting your request and have a strategy ready in advance to deal with it.

Situation 2

Steve has long hair and likes to wear it loose. The school rule states that long hair must be tied back during workshop lessons for safety reasons. Steve started work in the technology room without tying his hair back.

T   Steve, can I speak to you outside for a moment please?

S   Yes Miss?

T   You haven't tied your hair back. You know the rule for long hair don't you?

S   Yeah, but I can't be bothered.

T   Well, if you are going to continue you will have to observe the rule.

S   You're joking Miss. I've got mates who work in factories and they don't.

T   They may not (she agrees with him) but the rule applies here.

S   You can't make me.

T   You're right, I can't, but you are not working with it loose. (By asking him to go outside earlier, she is now in a strong position to prevent him returning. She stands across the doorway and physically bars his access.) So if you want to get back to work you'll have to tie your hair back. If not, you can sit out here in the corridor.

S   Yeah well, I think I'll do that. The work is boring anyway.

T   It's your choice, but the work will have to be done by the deadline otherwise … (She explains the consequences.)

The teacher left him and went back into the class. Steve eventually returned to the room with his hair tied back and the teacher offered help and began to rebuild the relationship. Steve made the choice. If he had decided not to return he would have had to face the consequences and that would be dealt with by the teacher later.

Swearing at another student

> The class is in small groups carrying out experiments. Part of the work involves a delicate operation. Suddenly one of the students stands up and swears loudly at someone in his group.

Your strategy

Working on topics in small groups can be a useful way of organizing the class so that the syllabus can be covered effectively. It enables the students to work collaboratively together and at the same time develop their interpersonal skills. Occasionally there will be disagreements and sometimes these are not resolved in an amicable way. When this happens you need to be on the spot and act as an arbiter to help the students work through their problem.

It is worth spending some time with the class discussing things like turn-taking and valuing the views and beliefs of others. Help them to develop ways of reaching decisions using a variety of methods including voting and going with the tide of enthusiasm to enable the work to proceed. Try them out with some 'what if' scenarios so that they can explore their own ideas on how to react when someone does not pull their weight, or lets the group down at the last minute, or starts an argument. This investment of time is well worth it as it will improve the management of group work in the long run.

Developing a code of practice

After these discussions, get each group to develop their own code of practice that they will agree to use. When a situation arises like the one described earlier, the students work through the problem, referring back to their code to identify what went wrong and why. They can then begin to repair the situation by agreeing what they will do in the future. This whole process should not take any longer than ten minutes and could be done during their free time.

Redirection

The difficulty of this approach is that the group will still have to work together for the rest of the lesson. You should step in and manage them during this time. Get them under control:

T   Sit down, Brian ... Sit down please.

S   Yes, but Sir he was ...

T   Sit down and be quiet.

S   It was Terry, Sir, he ...

T   Quiet please, I want to talk to all of you. (The teacher gives these two instructions to get order so that he can begin to resolve the problem. He does not get involved in who did what and who is to blame. When they are quiet he turns and addresses the whole class.)

T   Okay. I want everyone else to continue with your work.

(The aim is to get every student going again. There will probably be a few inquisitive students who will want to see what you will do next so you should try to minimise the 'show'. Turning to the group the teacher addresses them:)

T   I want to see you all at break (or at a convenient time later), and we will talk about what happened. But right now, you will all get back to work. Sally, show me where you got up to?

The teacher is letting them know that the incident will be dealt with, but at a more suitable time. He then redirects them all back to the task, and asks one of the students not involved to report on their progress. As Sally is describing their experiment, Terry interrupts:

Terry   It won't work that way, Sir.

Brian   'Course it will, you're so thick, even my little sister could see that, you pleb.

T   Brian, that's not very nice and we have an agreement in this school for respect and I expect you to use it.

Brian   Sorry Sir, but ... (The teacher stops him with a visual sign of the hand held up, palm facing Brian in the way a Police Officer will stop traffic).

T   Let's try the idea out anyway and see what will happen. If it does get stuck on the slope then at least you have tested the idea and can eliminate it. Designers often do this to satisfy themselves that they have chosen the best solution.

By doing it this way, the teacher prevents any further conflict. He cautions Brian about name-calling but also acknowledges that he has something to contribute that may be of value. He prepares the group for the possible failure by explaining that it is an important part of any experiment and is worth spending time on. He models the kind of behaviour that he wants them all to adopt.

Once the group are working together again you will be able to move away and check how the others are doing. If you do not feel confident then you may need to stay with them to the end of the lesson. When you see them after the lesson you should discuss what happened so the consequence of being held back is linked to the behaviour.

Swearing out loud in frustration

The class are working on their art projects and are using water-colour paints. One student is having difficulty with mixing the colours and as he reached over to dip his brush in the jar of water he dripped paint across his picture. 'Oh shit!' he exclaimed and then went quiet and just stared at his work.

Your strategy

People swear for various reasons and it is important to know the differences. The boy in this example is frustrated and expressing his feelings. His swearing is not directed at anyone and it is unlikely to upset. The best strategy is to tactically ignore it, especially if it is done quietly, and approach him and offer help. Later you could talk to him about what is acceptable in class, but at a more convenient time so as not to disturb the lesson.

Reminding about the rules

Swearing out loud so that the rest of the class can hear needs some kind of action. Discuss your proposed strategy with your colleagues so that you follow an agreed plan. Generally, swearing out of frustration needs a fairly unobtrusive response. Remind the student of the rule for swearing:

T   We have a rule for good language in class and I expect you to use it, Steven.

Finish with a smile and then see if you can help the student with what went wrong. Later you can discuss what he could do and say when he next gets annoyed with something. For example, you could suggest an inoffensive word that helps him vent his anger like 'Oh, sausages!'

You may hear a great deal of swearing and bad language in the playground during breaks and it would be futile and exhausting trying to pursue every single incident where frustration is the cause. Use your discretion to decide whether you think it will be useful to talk to a student who swears while he is playing. Certainly, there is a difference between their own games and those played during PE lessons where the teacher will be trying to teach the students the right kind of behaviour for the sport. When a student swears during an organised sporting activity taking place in a lesson you should call him over and remind him of the rule but do not stop the game, allow the other participants to continue.

Swearing at the teacher

> The class are working on a science project and one student starts misusing the apparatus and swinging a retort stand around. The teacher reprimands him for his foolish behaviour. He does not take it well and calls her a F★★★★★g cow!

Your strategy

The boy was clearly in the wrong swinging the piece of equipment around like a hammer. He was probably embarrassed at being caught and told off. He got aggressive and defiantly swore at her face so that everyone else could hear. If he had muttered it under his breath then tactically ignoring it is the best strategy, but make a point of picking it up later, out of the lesson.

It is important that we challenge abusive language so that students will know that it is unacceptable. When it happens in a way that is public, i.e. it is loud and blatantly directed at you in an aggressive way, be extremely assertive and serious and tell the student what he is doing wrong.

T   Phil, I don't talk to you like that and I don't expect you to talk like that to me.

Then discuss why he did it and help the student find a way to apologize. Talk about how to behave next time and remind him of the school rule on swearing.

Find out if your school has a policy on swearing and make sure you follow it. The practice may be to exit the student and to discuss the incident with him later. You do not have to take this kind of abuse and if you feel you are unable to deal with it confidently, seek the help of a more senior colleague.

A fight breaks out in the class

You have gone to great lengths to agree a code of behaviour with your students. You have regularly reminded them of it and it is fair to say that there is good order in your lessons. Then one day something unsuspected happens. The class are working in pairs on a task. You had your back to the students concerned because you were helping another group. Apparently one boy punched another and a fight broke out between them.

Your strategy

This is possibly one of our worst fears as teachers. When a fight breaks out in class it can be taken as a sign that the students are out of control and also that the teacher may not be able to manage the class. This is not always true. Fights occur in even the best schools and disagreements may come to a head anywhere in the school including the classroom. Students who lose their temper are showing they are unable to control their emotions and actions.

There are a number of things you could do in this situation depending on the circumstances. If the boys were big and brawny and you did not feel confident to tackle them you should send for help immediately. Either send a student to get the teacher from the nearest room or a senior member of staff. Then while you are waiting for help to arrive move the rest of the class back out of the way so they will be safe. Some fights are a 'windmill' of flailing arms and legs. They may also be quite mobile, especially if one of them is powerful and steams into the other thrusting him backwards. Most fights are over quickly. Usually, shouting out the names in a loud, assertive way followed by a short, direct instruction will be sufficient to stop the students fighting. For example:

T   Peter! To the Head's office. Now!

Get them apart by stepping between them when they stop. You may feel confident enough to split up a fight but never place yourself in any danger.

Most schools have an exit procedure and a supervised zone where students can be sent, so use it in these situations. If your school does not have a zone, send one of them to the school office with work to do. Then send for another teacher to collect the other child and take him back to his room to work. Later, you can work through what happened and why, and how the boys are going to repair the situation. In most schools, the deputy head or a senior teacher will deal with incidents like these so you should report it to them.

Follow school guidelines

An incident like this is dealt with a lot better if there is an agreed procedure in the school and strategies are thought out in advance. School guidelines on conflicts in the classrooms usually follow common procedures such as those listed below:

- Send a responsible student to get help.
- Ensure the safety of other students.
- Separate the students fighting as soon as you can.
- Send them to agreed isolation zones where they can be supervised; e.g. School office, Senior Teacher's office, a colleague's room nearby. They should take work to do with them.

- Report the incident to the Head or Deputy. (It is useful to make notes to avoid forgetting anything.)
- Discuss the incident with each student separately; even if the matter is handled by someone else. They are your students and will be coming back into your classroom.

Calm your class down

The other students in your class will be very unsettled. They may be excited, shocked, frightened or even feeling aggressive. You need to do something with them that will occupy their minds, slow them down, and have a calming effect. My own favourite is some dictation or a short period of copying notes from the board with key words missed out. These may not be your own preferred ways of teaching but they do result in a very quiet, busy class that can be controlled. Five to ten minutes will probably be enough time to get them all back to normal.

Bullying and name-calling

The class are doing a series of activities in order that you can assess their individual ability at PE. A group of students start laughing at one boy as he goes through the course and he gets very embarrassed and on the verge of tears. He carries on to the finish and then goes and stands on his own away from everyone.

Your strategy

Everyone in a school, students and staff alike, has the right to feel safe and be treated fairly by others. The organization of the school is based upon the acknowledgement of certain rights that everyone has and the responsibilities that accompany them. The school rules are the foundation of these rights and are there to ensure that everybody can co-exist and go about their business whether it is to learn, teach or support. When we join a school we agree to abide by its rules and also be responsible for upholding them. Codes of behaviour stem from the rules and provide a framework for protecting the rights of others. Ensuring your rights is my responsibility and vice versa.

At face value the scenario described seems like a very insignificant event of the kind that probably occurs frequently in most schools in this country. The victim is outnumbered and cannot defend himself very easily. He does not deserve such treatment.

The group who laughed at the boy for the way he did something was being hurtful and actually guilty of harassment. It may be that they did find his actions comical, but by laughing they were laughing at him, not with him. Making fun of him in a deliberate way, was infringing his right to learn. They were putting pressure on him to do something in a way that they approved of, and he may not have felt he was able to do it. The result would be that he did not attempt the activity at all for fear of failure. This is a form of bullying and must be addressed as soon as possible so that it does not get out of hand. You cannot afford to ignore it.

Follow school guidelines

Your school probably has guidelines for dealing with bullying, you should make sure you are familiar with them. The students will also have been made aware of them, and time spent explaining what harassment is, and why the school does not tolerate it, is well spent. The teachers will have discussed the issues and explained how important it is to treat others in the same way as we would like to be treated ourselves. Laughing and jeering at someone shows a lack of respect for the individual and their feelings.

Your approach

In our example, the teacher should go over and speak to the boy and find out what happened and why he is upset. If you already know because you saw the incident, still speak to him to get his story. Then arrange to see the other boys individually after the lesson. Make notes for comparison and do not commit yourself at this point even if they ask what it is about and what will happen to them.

Conflicts and dramas

Once you have all of their stories, decide whether you are going to handle it yourself or bring in a senior colleague to help. My advice is to go ahead with the minor incidents that require cautions, and formalise the serious ones that may lead to complaints and have more harmful effects on the victim.

Let things calm down and give yourself time to think them through, then act decisively by interviewing the boys again.

T   Michael, laughing at John in that way is spiteful. We have a school code for respect and you are expected to follow it.

S   Yes, but Sir it was just a bit of fun.

T   It was not much fun for John. You made him feel small and that hurts. We treat each other with respect here, so I expect you to do the same.

Most students will probably become apologetic at this point. A few may argue with you and deny it. Refocus them back onto the consequence of their action and the hurt they caused. Eventually they will realise they did wrong and be ready to apologize. The way to this needs patience, do not rush the student, give them time to think about the effects of their actions. Once they have owned up, you can move to a stage of repairing the situation.

In the same way that young first offenders are being made by the police to meet their victim and experience, first-hand, the results of their crime, you can bring the victim into contact with the boys so he can tell them what it felt like to be laughed at in that way. The outcome of the process should be a debriefing with the boys to establish what they are going to do to put things right and what they will do in the future to prevent such an event re-occurring.

Sexist remarks between students

> The students are sitting in pairs facing each other, four to a table. They are engaged in a graphics project that is particularly challenging. A girl raises her hand. She complains that the boys opposite are upsetting her friend by saying her drawing is rubbish and that girls are no good at it. She has stopped drawing and is crying.

Your strategy

Sexist remarks of this kind are unacceptable in the classroom and must be addressed immediately. They are another form of harassment and, as in this case hurtful and detrimental to learning. The classroom needs to be a place where everyone can learn and the prejudices of society are not reinforced. The difficulty the teacher has in this example is in deciding who is telling the truth. This should not be attempted during the lesson because the rest of the class need attention as well. The teacher needs to resolve the problem of the students working at the same table.

Your approach

The best solution is to move both the girl and the two boys to new seats if that is possible. The instruction to move needs to be made carefully.

T   Mark, Tony, Jane ... clearly there seems to be a bit of a problem here. I will see each of you at the end of the lesson, but for the time being I want to move all of you so you can get on with your work. Now ... Jane here, Mark here and Tony over here.

The teacher is acknowledging that there is something wrong but not apportioning any blame. She is letting them know she is taking it seriously by discussing it later with them. This signals to them that the work comes first and that is why she is moving them. They are all given new places as a sign that they are all equal and no one is carrying more of the blame. They are all implicated which is why they are moving. She does not wait for an agreement or listen to any protests, instead she turns away and starts helping some other students. She is expecting them to do what she says and is giving them time for it to sink in. If after a few minutes they have not moved she will return and continue ...

T   Jane, I asked you to move and I expect your co-operation. But if you feel you cannot move to that place you may sit at my desk with me. Now make your mind up so that I can help you get started.

She turns away again, expecting the student to change places. Jane probably feels more willing because she has a choice and can own her actions. The reason the teacher did not offer them all a choice right from the start was because she wanted them to see that she was taking the incident seriously and the first consequence of their action was to lose the right to sit together where they wanted. The choice offered to Jane would get a decision because it returns the power to decide to the student. The option of sitting at the teacher's desk is not very appealing so she goes for the one that was originally offered. You could of course use this option right from the start.

Once the students are settled in their new places the teacher returns and offers to help with the work. The girl in particular needs extra attention because she cannot start the work. During a move like this you could make sure the 'victim' has the things she needs and when she is settled make some positive comments about her work so that she feels confident about her progress so far.

At the end of the lesson remind them that you would like to see them so you can get to the bottom of the story and resolve it. The boys may try to make it all sound like a bit of fun so remind them that jokes that are personal, hurt.

A student bursts into tears because of the work

> Sometimes the pupils find the work we give them particularly challenging and requiring a high level of concentration and effort. On one occasion the class were enjoying the challenge and were very absorbed, except one student who had a sad expression on her face. When the teacher tried to talk to her she burst into tears and said she did not understand the problem and could not do it.

Your strategy

This can be extremely difficult because it would be easy for the teacher to take it personally, as she set the work that may cause the student to feel this way. Being a teacher is a very difficult job, make the wrong decision and you may ruin a child's enthusiasm for the subject.

The girl in this scenario is not being prevented from doing the work, but there is a barrier to her getting on with it. She is bright and able, so careful handling of the situation will enable her to see where she is having difficulty and sort out a way through it. Be gentle with her, she is probably having a bad day, we all have those now and then! Work on the basis that she can do it.

Your approach

Kneel down so you are at her level, smile, and make a practical suggestion:

T   Sally ... come on now, let me see if I can help.
     (Pause for a few seconds and turn her book so you can see what she has done.)
T   Now let's see if we can do this together. Dry your eyes while I see what you have to do.

This approach employs the same strategy of expecting the child to do something as I have discussed earlier, by picking up the book and looking at it while she dries her eyes, you can give her some take-up time. When she is ready you continue.

T   So, the task is to estimate what the answer will be which means you have to round the numbers to the nearest 10. So what will 57 be ... ?

S   60.

T   Very good (said with emphasis and a smile), and how about 84?

S   80.

T   That's right, now you know how to multiply units of 10 in your head don't you?

S   Yes Miss (she is gaining confidence).

T   Right, you complete that one. Then do the other three estimations. When you have finished, raise your hand and I will come back and see how you got on and help you start the next section. All right?

The teacher takes her through the work and praises her to build her confidence and self-esteem. Eventually her confidence begins to return but the teacher stays with her as she nears the end. Once the teacher is happy that she knows what to do she can be left with the knowledge that the teacher will return when she needs to start the next section. She was more than able to do the work but the size of the task may have been putting her off.

This is often a barrier to learning for students. They know how to do the things within an assignment or task but they do not have very well developed skills in breaking it down into its smaller constituent parts. They see it as an enormous problem because they cannot see how it is made up. It is important to structure the work in a way that develops this skill as well as developing their knowledge of the subject. Problem solving is a valuable, transferable skill, and is worth cultivating and teaching because it is the foundation for learning.

A student has a nosebleed during the lesson

> The lesson is progressing well, the students are working hard and it has been an uneventful morning when suddenly a girl comes out to you with her face covered with blood. She has a bad nosebleed and the sight of blood is beginning to make the other students panic.

Your strategy

Nosebleeds look worse than they actually are, but they need careful attention to stop the bleeding. Firstly, get some tissues or clean cloth and make a fairly large compress. Place it gently over the girl's nose and ask her to hold it there. Then send her to the school office where she can be looked after and first aid administered to stop the bleeding.

Your responsibility lies with your class and ensuring they are supervised. Once the girl has left the room you can quickly clean any spots of blood off the floor, desks and chairs. (You should inform the cleaners later so that the area can be disinfected).

Calm your class down

Now you can begin to calm the class. This needs to be done quickly and without fuss so that they can return to work. Once they have something to occupy their thoughts they will quickly settle again. Your approach could be:

T   Right everyone, pay attention to me please. (Spoken in a friendly manner with a smile.) Jennifer will be all right, she has a nosebleed and it will stop soon. She will probably be back with us after break. Now this seems to be a good time to …

You go on to conduct a whole class activity. Depending on their age and what they were doing you could hold a five minutes arithmetic or spelling test. If you do, pitch it low enough so that they get the answers right to restore their confidence after the shock.

A student is sick during the lesson

Halfway through the lesson one of the students is suddenly sick. Luckily, he vomits onto the floor away from the others. There is a terrible stench in the room and the aisle between the desks is splattered. He is looking very pale and sorry for himself and the other students nearby are beginning to over-react by holding their noses and feigning asphyxiation.

Your strategy

This is one of the situations that tests teachers to their limit. There is a sick boy to sort out, the room to clear up and the other children to control and restore order. Young children give little warning of their feelings. Everything may be progressing well and then suddenly the class is in turmoil. You need to think and act clearly. When a child complains that they feel sick it is important that they are taken seriously. Children who tell you they have a stomach-ache or feel queasy will either want to go to the toilet or be sick. If this happens arrange for the child to be escorted to an appropriate place where he can be supervised and nursed if the need arises.

Sometimes you will get no warning and the child is sick before you can do anything. When this happens, act quickly. You cannot afford to leave your class for the sake of one child because the others will need you and you will have to supervise them while the room is cleaned. Get one of the sensible children in the class to escort the boy to the school secretary immediately. It is worth keeping a bucket handy for this eventuality so that there will be less to clear up if the child is sick on the way. Send a message with them for the caretaker to come and clear up the mess. Then move your class to another room, the library or any space available where they can be seated for the remainder of the lesson. Read them a story, have a quiz or do something that will usefully occupy them. You will probably have to abandon your original lesson plan because a disruption like this is very difficult to ride through. The change of rooms and the novelty of the event will be too much for the children.

Your main aim is to remove them from the room so it can be cleaned and to maintain order till the lesson finishes.

The sick child may not return to the lesson so you should try to get in touch with his parents and enquire how he is. This will enable you to find out what was wrong with him and how long he will be off school. You can discuss sending homework with them so he will not fall behind. Remember to thank the child who escorted him and perhaps even give a little reward such as a house point, star, sticker or whatever system you use in your school.

Textbooks get damaged or lost

> Last lesson you gave every student a new textbook and asked that they take good care of them and keep them safe. Walking around the classroom, you notice that one student's book has a dilapidated appearance and a torn cover. Books are expensive and you cannot replace them easily so they must be looked after. Careless use needs to be addressed.

Your strategy

One of the problems that many teachers have is the care and preservation of sets of books. A generous budget and poor management can lead to an 'easy come, easy go' situation where resources are not valued highly.

There needs to be strict control of the issuing and return of books and this is the responsibility of the teacher. Heads of department should monitor stocks on an annual basis and request explanations for losses and damages. In this way resources will be valued and the ever decreasing sums of money that schools receive can be used wisely rather than wasted on continually replacing things.

Your approach

The problem of the student with the damaged book should not be dealt with in the lesson as you will distract her from her work. Go over to her and whisper:

T Will you see me at the end of the lesson please, Rebecca?

Make it a friendly request so as not to cause her any worry.

When you do talk to her at the end in privacy, first find out how the cover got torn, because it may have been an accident that was unavoidable.

T I see that the cover of your book is torn. How did it happen?

S Miss, my younger brother got hold of it and chewed the corners. I tried to get it away from him and he held onto it and the cover got ripped. I'm sorry, Miss.

T We cannot have books getting damaged like this. I shall be writing home to your parents about it. But in the meantime, I would like you to cover it until it can be repaired.

S Okay Miss.

T ... and Rebecca. You need to look after your books if you have a toddler in your house. Only get them out when he is not around and always put them away when you are finished. All right?

S Yes Miss.

Finish with a smile to show her you are not cross as it was not all her fault.

You may not be satisfied with her explanation so the suggestion of a letter home may well prompt the student to change her story. If she does not, you will be able to talk it over with the parents and if the damage was caused by negligence you will be able to discuss the difficulties of maintaining books, and possibly even seek some kind of financial remuneration.

Students submit almost identical homework

Working through a set of books you are suddenly struck by the similarity of two pieces of homework. Upon closer examination you realise that they are almost the same and conclude that they either worked together or one og them has copied the work.

Your strategy

Many teachers use group work to enable the sharing of ideas and the contributions made by each student are assimilated and become part of the final piece of work. The trouble with this practice is that it becomes hard to separate out who did what.

Students can keep a log of what they did. Alternatively they can evaluate the work of the group and describe how they contributed to the project. They can focus on how their efforts have led to the success of the group, and provide opportunities to reflect on things they need to improve on. The log and evaluation are assessable outcomes and can carry considerable weight in the final grading of the project.

The assessment procedure usually involves awarding each member of the group the same grade for the project and individual grades for their evaluations. They are unlikely to submit evaluations that are the same because they will have made their own unique contributions, and have formed their own opinions.

Teachers need to be able to differentiate between close collaboration and copying, if the work looks similar and has not been done in a group situation. Oral questioning to test individual understanding is a useful way of differentiating between collaboration and copying. Arrange to see the students concerned before you give them back their work, and talk to them individually:

T   That was a good piece of work you submitted on the characters in Macbeth. Did someone help you or did you do it all yourself?

S   I did it on my own, Miss. Why, what is wrong with it?

T   Nothing, but in order that I can give it the grade it deserves I need to ask you a few questions to help me understand what you are trying to say.

The student is given a chance to say whether she worked with someone else, but if she denies it you do not accuse her. Instead, try testing whether they know what they have been writing about. Both students may answer your questions satisfactorily, in which case you can grade their work and say nothing else. If they have tried to cheat, they will know you have detected it and will think twice in the future.

If one of the students cannot answer the questions to your satisfaction it indicates that she has probably leaned rather heavily on her friend to complete the work. Challenge the student and see whether they own up to it:

T   I am unhappy about the work you submitted. It would seem that you do not have a good grasp of what you have been writing about. Furthermore your work shows more than a coincidental similarity to … ! It is my belief that you shared the work, or maybe even copied it. Do you have anything to say?

She will probably be too embarrassed and may even break down in tears, so be prepared. When she has replied, outline what you expect from her:

T   I regard copying, or plagiarism as it is called, as an extremely serious matter and cannot allow it to go unnoticed. To spare you any public embarrassment I am going to offer you the chance to make amends.

Then either set the student a similar task to complete by an agreed deadline in her own time or get her to sit an examination that covers the work. The object of the exercise is to find out what the student knows and show her that there is no profit in cheating.

Summary

Managing situations that can occur at any time requires quick thinking. The teacher who is able to act appropriately when, and where, he or she is needed, will bring order and calm back to the situation. The kind of immediate response that is required comes from experience and some pre-empting, or advance planning, of possible events. New teachers probably will not have had sufficient experience of many of the problems in this chapter. Sharing experience and talking about ways of resolving these dilemmas will help. Agreeing a set of procedures for some of the more serious or delicate incidents like bullying, fighting and medical related problems will ensure all staff act in the same way and can support each other.

Key points for managing conflicts and dramas

- Deal with 'resistant' students away from their peer group to avoid enhancing their status and turning them into 'martyrs'.
- Teach groups how to resolve their own differences of opinion by using democratic methods to reach decisions.
- Use unobtrusive strategies to deal with frustrated students who swear.
- Act decisively when a student swears at or is rude to a teacher. Allow the student to cool off, then talk to him or her about your expectations.
- Never place yourself in danger when a fight occurs. Enlist help and use non-physical methods to split up the students.
- Deal with harassment by encouraging bullies to empathise with their victims as a means of gaining a satisfactory solution, and an apology.
- Offer ways out for students who bully, harass or swear because they think it is a joke. However, serious offenders must be formally dealt with and punished.
- Never leave your class to accompany children with minor sickness or nosebleeds, always send them to a pre-arranged point like the school office.
- If you feel students have copied work check whether they understand what they have submitted by oral testing.

4

BEYOND THE CLASSROOM

Introduction

The job of a teacher extends beyond the classroom to include ensuring the safety and good behaviour of the students while they are in the school. We take on this responsibility regardless of whether we are on duty or not, because it is a part of our role as professional teachers. Furthermore, it is in our interest to maintain good behaviour outside the lessons, as well as during them because it will have a knock-on effect in the classroom. A well-disciplined school environment is conducive to effective learning.

The playground offers a place for students to let off steam after less physically demanding activities in the classroom. Children can organise their own games and pastimes, but playgrounds can become difficult places to be in for some individuals. It is important to stand back and give children the freedom to express themselves, but at the same time remain vigilant and on the lookout for any bullying and aggressive behaviour that could escalate if it is not nipped in the bud.

Schools are often judged by the behaviour of their students in public places. Uniforms make the students particularly conspicuous, and so we need to make sure the values of the school are upheld. Rowdiness, swearing, fighting, bullying, dropping litter and looking scruffy are things that are particularly noticeable and are used to label the school as 'poor' or 'rough'. These kinds of behaviour should become the primary concern of all staff if the reputation of the school is to be improved.

This chapter presents a range of strategies for some typical problems that occur outside the classroom: in corridors, playgrounds and beyond the school gates. They include: bullying, fighting, being abusive to teachers outside school, defacing school property and being a nuisance while waiting for buses. The emphasis is on finding ways to resolve the problems without getting into conflict situations.

Moving rooms, and distractions in corridors

There is an exceptionally high number of boisterous students in one of your classes. You have planned a lesson that requires moving the class to the computer room which is located at the other end of the corridor. How can you move them quickly and quietly with the minimum of fuss?

Your strategy

Secondary schools and Further Education (FE) colleges can be like railway stations at times, with people moving about in all directions as they find their way to their next lessons, chattering and larking around as they go. The noise and activity is very disruptive to the classes that are continuing through the bell. Sometimes it is almost impossible to carry on because the students are easily distracted after an hour of sitting in the same room with the same people. You need to be patient and wherever possible use a little humour. We will return to this later, but first let us look at ways of minimising the disturbance students may cause as they move down the corridor.

Your approach with younger children

The main disturbance to other classes will be noise, so brief your class about it in advance. You will have two options at the start of a lesson; either talk to them in the corridor or let them into the room and then talk to them. Giving instructions in the corridor is difficult unless you raise your voice because thirty children will not always stand in an orderly, quiet line. You will have to gain their attention without disturbing classes nearby, and you will probably end up making more noise than the students will make walking down the corridor.

Get the class into the room and settled as quickly as possible. They will know how to behave in your room so you can give them instructions more easily. Tell them where they will be going, what they will be doing and why. This will prevent any questions on the way. Once the class have stowed coats, bags, and got books and equipment they need, you can make a start. You may use a reward system to encourage the behaviour you want.

T   It is very important that everyone in this class is well behaved during the walk from here to the computer room. When I give the sign, we go into silent mode. Let's imagine we are on a secret mission and the slightest sound will give us away to the other side. I will give one house point to all those who are absolutely silent until I give the all-clear sign in the computer room. Do you all understand?

The teacher's strategy is a clever one for the age group. She is offering everyone in the class a chance to earn a reward. It is a team operation not a competition. She could have made it a competition but what would she have done if they had all been silent? If she ended up giving them all rewards, then she might as well have offered them all the chance to begin with. Also, some children do not respond to competitive situations because they do not perceive themselves as winners.

When everyone is ready, give the sign to leave. Stand at the door, half in the room so you have a view of the corridor as well. You may wish to have a brief word with any children you feel may find it difficult to be quiet or sensible. Once inside the new room, get the class to their seats and if they have been successful in doing as you asked give them plenty of praise as well as their rewards.

Your approach with older students

Older students are more challenging, and you may not be able to use the same reward system. Brief them in advance in the same way, and then send them off in pairs, leaving a few seconds before the next pair go. Again, remind poor behavers of what you expect before they leave the room. You could offer them a reward, such as five minutes trying out some of the games software or a similar treat related to your subject or room. Make the reward accessible to all the students and something they will value that is not out of proportion to what is being asked of them.

Managing a class working through the bell

You have a problem with a group of older students gathering outside your room, chatting and larking about. The most effective strategy is to go out and have a few words with them.

T   Hi lads. I am still in the middle of a lesson here and you are disturbing my students. I know you are only having a chat so could you either go to the canteen or the common room. Thanks.

Turn away and go back into your room with the expectation that they will move on. The key is to approach them in a non-threatening way by smiling and using open gestures. You should recognise that they probably do not know they are doing anything wrong. Finish by offering them a choice of places to go to. They will be more likely to co-operate if they can own their own decision. You may get one or two comments from the cheeky ones but you should tactically ignore them and if necessary, reiterate the choices. This avoids any possible confrontation and you can return to your lesson.

The more common approach is to open the door and bellow at the students. This may work with younger children but it will cause problems with the older ones. Larger groups may require you to raise your voice but if there are only a few children it is not necessary and actually reinforces a particularly harsh kind of behaviour. It is better to save the shouting for the serious occasions.

Sometimes students loiter outside rooms during their free periods. They signal to their friends in the class and distract them from their work. The only way to stop them is to go out and ask them to leave. It disrupts the lesson, but if you ignore them they will stay. Prevention is the best deterrent, so if you are timetabled in a room facing a busy corridor, tell the students in your class to have a word with their friends and ask them to wait somewhere else.

Defacing school noticeboards

On your way to your classroom you notice two students defacing a poster in one of the rooms. They do not see you because you are outside in the playground and they have their backs to the windows. You do not teach them yourself but you know their names. What should you do?

Your strategy

This particular example is complicated by the fact that you are outside the building. Had you been inside you could have dealt with them immediately, but you cannot do it from the outside. You may be tempted to rap on the window, but they are likely to run away and then it will be hard to get them to own up. You really need to get to the room and catch them at it if you can. This may be difficult if the school is a large one. You may also have other things to attend to. However, vandalism and the disregard for school property needs to be made a priority so you should try to deal with it if you can.

Make your way to the room and enter it immediately. The students will probably turn around and act innocently. Get them to sit down somewhere away from the posters and avoid asking them what they were doing, as you will probably get a series of tales and excuses. There are several strategies you can try depending on the circumstances. Your school may have a rule about being in rooms unsupervised at break and lunchtimes, and so you will be able to use it to open the discussion. The school may allow students in the rooms and have codes for their proper use, so begin from this point.

While the students are sitting you can survey the extent of their actions. If it is negligible just talk to them about the amount of effort that goes into wall displays. Cleverly talking around the incident and engaging in direct eye contact at the points where you refer to the need to prevent deliberate damage will communicate to them that you know what they were doing. For example:

T   I was walking past this room a few minutes ago and I saw you doing something (make eye contact) to the wall displays. It takes a lot of effort to put them up and make the rooms pleasant for you (again, direct eye contact). It reminds me of a display that needs changing. I would appreciate it if you would both help me with it.

The teacher has not accused either of them directly because she feels that it would be a hard one to prove. Instead, she goes for a solution that will enable them to see how much work is involved and give them some ownership of a school display board.

When the damage is obvious, challenge them and get them to own up.

T   As I passed this room a few minutes ago I saw you both at the back by that poster (pointing to the damage).
S   It wasn't us, Miss.
T   It was someone. That is a deliberate act of vandalism. These obscene words have been written during break. We can easily prove it wasn't either of you by comparing the handwriting and pens you have with the writing on the poster. Do you understand? (making eye contact again).
S   Yes, but it wasn't us, we were just reading them.
T   Maybe you were. So I am going to offer you a choice. You can empty your pockets and we shall compare your pens and writing with the writing on the poster. If it proves to be yours we shall ask your parents to come in so we can discuss this. I am sure they will be furious if they were to see what you have written ... or you can own up to it now and I will not say anything to them.

The teacher is using parental disapproval and the punishment they may impose at home as the threat and then offering them a way out if they do the right thing. When they own up to what they did they will face a lesser consequence.

Once they have owned up you can begin to work with them on 'repairing' their actions. You might try getting them to help you or a colleague to put up a display, and then offering them the responsibility for taking care of it. This may involve checking for damage and deterioration, and repairing and repinning where necessary. You could set a limit of a week or even a month for this job, but make sure you give praise if it is done well. Younger students feel very important if they get a title like 'Display Monitor'.

The punishment or consequence is made to fit the wrongdoing. The students will have to give up their time, but in return they may come to take pride in the work especially if it will make them feel important. Then they are less likely to repeat the offence again.

Bullying on the way to school

During break duty a sixth form student comes and asks if she can have a private word about her friend Panna. It seems that Panna is getting bullied on the bus by some upper school boys and several sixth formers. She is not English and does not have a very good grasp of the language which makes it hard for her to stand up for herself. She has started arriving late at school and seems tearful at times.

Your strategy

The primary role of the school is to educate the students. This is an extremely complex task and involves much more than just what goes on in the classroom. How far should the role of the teacher extend? Whatever your view, if a student feels they cannot come to school because of problems faced on the journey then the teacher needs to intervene to find a solution.

This example is complicated in a number of ways. The girl's lack of English was causing her to struggle with her coursework because it required her to have reasonable spoken and written language skills. Her confidence was low so she became an easy target for children who got pleasure exploiting people's weaknesses by bullying and ridiculing them. She felt unable to answer back, and probably did not feel strong enough to do so.

A further investigation found other incidents of harassment on the bus since the start of term. When the register was examined a clear pattern of lateness emerged. Panna explained that she had stopped using the school bus and was coming by another route on the town bus. One of her support teachers got the names of the boys involved from her. Panna eventually broke down and burst into tears. She felt she could no longer carry on and was giving up school. She went on to reveal that she was not living with her parents anymore. She had rented a room and was involved in a dispute with the landlord over the heating.

The situation was a sensitive one and needed to be handled with extreme care and sensitivity. However it is dealt with it is vital that the bullying stops.

Not all children who bully are weak and irresponsible. Sometimes they are just thoughtless and insensitive. They go along with it because they want to belong to the group or gang. This leads to trouble for some of the most unlikely children. Identifying them from the rest can be important because they are the ones who will be the most receptive and listen to reason. They will see the harm they have caused and feel remorse.

Your approach

In Panna's case, one of the perpetrators was offered the extremely important job of watching out for her on the bus, and if any further bullying occurred he was to intervene. It looked like the problem would be solved and she would use the bus again. Then Jane, a year 11 girl, complained that she was being bullied by some sixth form girls because of something that had happened on the bus. She claimed that they had threatened her if she went anywhere near Panna again, but she said she had not touched her.

Jane was told that the school was fully aware of the situation and it was being dealt with. she was asked to stay out of it and in return a teacher would talk to the sixth formers and get them to back off and not use vigilante methods. Jane agreed. Meanwhile, Panna had heard that the sixth formers were going to be punished for sticking up for her so she went to her tutor and asked her to prevent it. The tutor spoke to the teacher who re-assured her that he would not be punishing them but would be talking to them.

The sixth form girls were called to a meeting:

T   Can I begin by thanking you for your concern. It is admirable, and Panna appreciates your loyalty in sticking up for her. The school is aware of the problem and the Head interviewed the boys and girls involved.

S   Yes, but that's not going to stop it and I'm not going to sit back and let them do it again.

T   We have taken steps to prevent it happening again.

S   No one listens to teachers. I had to comfort Panna for nearly an hour. She was really upset and worried and that's why I told that year 11 girl that if she came near Panna again she would be dead meat!

T   You can't take the law into your own hands and ...

S   We have to, Sir, 'cos they're not going to take any notice of teachers. But if a sixth former says something they will. When I was younger we were afraid of the sixth form students. If they told me to get lost or something I would because I was s**t scared!

T   Let me tell you what I have done. I have asked Colin Smith (a sixth former) to look after her on the bus and if anyone tries anything he will intervene.

S   (The student raises her eyebrows and laughs.) He's one of the ones doing the bullying!

T   I know, that's why I asked him. We discussed the whole thing and he understood how she must have felt. I explained that the job was very important and it placed a great responsibility on him and he rose to the challenge. So you see, I have done what you are suggesting.

S   I suppose so (she is stopped in her tracks by this), but if it don't work I'm gonna get them.

T   Promise me you will give my way a chance.

S   All right.

T   And if anything happens, see me before you take it on yourself, deal?

S   Okay.

The teacher cunningly turned the situation around because he had anticipated the student view in these kinds of situations. Through all discussions he tactfully ignored the secondary squabbles between the students and kept the attention and action focused on Panna.

Playground argy-bargy

> Walking round the playground during break duty you become aware of a group of students acting suspiciously. They are surrounding a younger student jeering at him. You pause and watch for a minute and then approach. They seem to be tormenting the boy about his bike and he is almost in tears.

Your strategy

Playgrounds can be jungles where only the strongest survive. Children are free to run around and let off steam, engaging in games and sports and creating fantastic, imaginary stories of their own. They have up to an hour of structure-free recreation that punctuates the lessons at lunchtime, with several shorter breaks in the morning and sometimes afternoon. It is fascinating to watch them and see how they use their imagination. Some students take advantage of the absence of adults and assume positions of power. Micro-societies and gangs emerge and distinct pecking orders become established. Schools with more than one playground separate the older students from the younger ones to minimise this, but incidents may still occur, and you need to talk to those involved to establish whether it is just everyday argy-bargy or something more serious.

Teachers hold positions of authority and the power that goes with the job, but they have a limited number of sanctions to maintain order. There is an increasing need for psychological strategies (hence the need for this book) because corporal punishment and threats are unacceptable. Nevertheless, the teacher does have the authority to do what the school expects. A teacher can insist that he interviews a student about his behaviour. It is the way this is achieved that we are considering here. The teacher can insist that rules are upheld so that everyone in the school is safe and free from abuse and harassment. You are in charge, and you have to send out the right messages to the other students in the playground. Your position has several weaknesses; you are on their territory (the playground) and you are not in a position to make a judgement because you do not have everyone's story. Find out the facts, but avoid getting drawn into a discussion.

Your approach

It may be difficult to identify the students involved especially if it is a large school, so ask students nearby to tell you the names of one or two of them before you approach. Then walk decisively up to the group. Do not get involved in a conversation by asking what is going on as it will only result in a host of replies all saying 'nothing'. Your objective is to remove the younger student from the situation and then talk to the older students.

T   Good afternoon boys. This looks like an interesting meeting. Now, (turning to the young boy), what's your name?

S   Michael, Sir.

T   Well Michael, will you go and tell the secretary that I will be needing some new board pens this afternoon (or any other prearranged errand for this kind of incident) and wait there because I want to see you.

Send the young boy off on the errand and make sure you talk to him and get his story. Then deal with the others.

T   I don't know what is going on here so I want you all to go to my room now please.

Be insistent, and once you have them in the room get them each to write an account of what was going on. Do this immediately so they do not have any time to work on their stories. Do not accuse them of anything but remind them to be accurate as you will be comparing their versions with the younger boy's story.

T   If I find that you have missed something important out, or you have lied, I shall assume you have something to hide. This is a serious matter and the best thing you can do to help yourself now is to be honest.

This will get most students to tell the truth and they will be disloyal and 'rat' on each other because they will not want to shoulder the blame themselves. The ringleader may also be seduced into believing that a confession will get him off. Do the same with the younger boy.

Dealing with bullying

A comparison of the versions will enable you to ascertain whether it is just playground argy-bargy, or something more serious. If it is the former, give them a ticking off and warn them that you will be telling the younger boy to come straight to you if it happens again. Advise them that their best bet is to stay clear of him in future. However, you may decide that it is a serious matter and want to refer it on, so let them know that you will want to talk to them again later on. Bullying is often an offence that results in exclusion and so the Deputy, or the Head, will have to have the final say. If it does go that far, observe how they deal with it because Headteachers will probably have had experience of it before and you can learn a lot from them.

Disputes during playground games

Ball games are very popular and they are usually played safely and without incident. However on one occasion, while hurrying back to the staffroom for a quick 'cuppa', your attention is drawn to two older students shouting at each other. It seems that one of the boys had made a dangerous tackle and now they are facing up to each other and tempers are rising.

Your strategy

Boisterous games in the playground often lead to clashes but in most cases they do not come to anything and the game continues. Occasionally they flare up and fights break out because there is a feud between the students that has deeper roots. When they find themselves on opposite sides in a game of football the situation worsens. The slightest chance is taken and retaliation occurs.

Situation 1

In this example the boys look like they are going to take the matter further, and need to be stopped. Playgrounds are noisy places so there is little chance of you being heard if you try to shout a warning to stop. Get closer to make yourself heard then call out their names:

T   Mark! Steven!

This will get their attention, and let them know you are watching and in charge. Alternatively, you could use a whistle. Once you have their attention take control of the situation.

T   Steven, over there (pointing to the far end of the playground), and Mark, over there (pointing to the opposite end).

When you have separated them, go to the nearest boy and talk to him.

Disputes during playground games

T   What was going on there?

S   Nothing, Sir.

T   Okay, go in and wait outside my room and cool off. I shall be in to talk to you in a few minutes.

Do the same with the other boy and accompany him. When you reach your room invite the boy who has been waiting in and talk to him. Find out about the incident from both boys by asking them to write down what happened. This will allow them time to cool down, and give you something to make comparisons with, and if the dispute is part of a more serious problem you can pass the notes on. The bottom line will be that fighting is not tolerated, and starting fights breaks this rule and must lead to a consequence.

Situation 2

Children are usually very good at refereeing their own games and will know when a game rule is broken. Occasionally someone may try and get away with something and then a dispute will occur. You will come across such disputes during playground duty and the best approach is to intervene. If you actually witnessed the incident act as the referee:

T   Right, Michael, that was a dangerous tackle, so the other team get a free-kick. Move back ten feet please. John (hand the ball to him), take a free-kick here please (pointing to the spot).

S   When, Sir?

T   Wait a moment, back a bit further, Michael, and keep it clean please. Okay, ready when you are, John.

The whole thing is dealt with quickly and fairly and the free-kick gets the game moving. Wait and watch for a few minutes to make sure the boys are playing fairly, perhaps you may even call out some tactical comments and words of praise and then depart.

Situation 3

You need a different approach when you do not see what has happened. With ball games like football it is fairly easy to settle things. A colleague of mine used to walk into the area of play, and gain the attention of the student with the ball.

T   Colin! Stop please and bring the ball here.

He made sure he had been heard and Colin stopped, then he went over to the boys who were arguing.

T   Stop this immediately.
S   Yes, but Sir he ...
T   Stop please, this is a game.
S   But Sir ... (one boy persists in his effort to explain).
T   Boys, I am going to give you both a fair chance. I will bounce-up (this is done by getting them to face each other, then the ball is either bounced or tossed up between them and play continues). I want it to be a fair challenge and let's have no more arguing, okay?
S   Yes Sir (together).
T   Right, face up.

This method of restarting a game after a dispute is acceptable because it is widely used in professional matches.

You may want to talk to the students about their behaviour. It can be done by removing them from the game, restarting it in the same way with two other players and then having a few words about good sportsmanship. It is best to resolve the situation quickly and quietly because the chances are that a fresh start will end the problem.

Dropping litter in the playground

It is nearly the end of the lunchbreak and you are following a group of students along the drive towards the classrooms. They are chatting, eating and drinking as they walk. When they reach the entrance, they finish their snacks and some of them throw their litter on the ground. There is no rule about litter but the student handbook does state the need to care for the school environment.

Your strategy

Litter is unsightly, and at times dangerous, so students should be made aware of their responsibility. There are a number of ways for trying to get them to pick it up. An aggressive approach may work because the students are scared of you or it will fail because they will take umbrage at being spoken to in that way. Both lead to negative feelings, so another method is required.

First gain their attention, then ask them to come back to where you are standing. Do it in a friendly way by smiling and using first names if you can, then begin by stating the school's position:

T We don't drop litter in the school grounds. It is unsightly and a health hazard. I followed you, and saw you drop that sweet wrapper and that tin. Will you pick them up and put them in the bin, please. (End with a smile, turn away and go in.)

Do not stand and wait to see if they do what you asked. Smile and thank them for their co-operation and walk away. Take a look back over your shoulder and if they are showing no signs of picking the litter up, turn back:

T I asked you politely to pick up your litter but you have not done it. Please do it now so we can all get to registration on time.

Linger a bit longer at the entrance and chat to other students keeping a casual eye on them to check they do as you ask.

Choosing the consequences

If the students still don't do as requested, target them by name:

T   Colin and Naomi, come here please.
S   Yes Sir (sulkily).
T   That is your litter, either pick it up or come to my room immediately after registration. Thank you.

This shows others looking on that you have not let the students get the better of you, and you will be taking more serious action if they do not do you ask. They have a choice, and can own their own decision, either to choose the cleaning up option or the consequence. In most cases the students will accept that they have to tidy up and will do it.

Riding bicycles in the school playground

At home-time the students bustle and jostle to the school gate where you are on duty. A number of them get their bikes and walk them to the gate. A little while later a boy comes out, gets his bike and pedals furiously to try to catch up his friends. The rule is that bikes must not be ridden in the school grounds.

Your strategy

Riding a bike across a busy playground can be dangerous to both the children walking and the rider. For example, if a ball game is going on and the rider gets hit by the ball he may go out of control and crash. That is why schools insist that cyclists wheel their bikes out of the grounds.

In this example, the boy is riding to catch his friends up and is not taking as much care as he should. It is not necessary to shout because he is coming to the gate. Move towards him so you can be seen and raise your hand to indicate that you want him to stop. He may realise what he is doing and get off immediately so all you need to do is have a few words with him about riding in the playground.

Reminding about the rules

When he reaches you, begin with a friendly remark:

T   Nice bike.
S   Thank you, Sir.
T   We have a rule about cycling in the school. Do you know it?
S   No Sir (he replies cheekily).
T   You walk your bicycle in the school grounds.
S   Right Sir.
T   Thank you.

Your opening comment shows you are not cross and will be fair. A compliment about the student's bike or personal possessions often throws them a bit, and helps defuse the situation. Ascertaining whether the student knows the rule enables you to decide if it was broken deliberately or not. The teacher in this example ignores the cheeky reply and takes it as a genuine answer so that he can explain the rule. He resists the temptation of arguing that the cyclists may have been reminded of the rule previously, because it will not help reach the objective which is to ensure he knows the rule and wheels his bike. You may have had to do this before, so simply remind him and let him know you are noting the event and will be putting it in his file. A further infringement of this rule may lead to him being banned from bringing his bike into the school.

Bus queues and bad behaviour

It's bus duty and the end of term is looming. The general standard of behaviour is deteriorating because the students are either getting excited about the holidays, or looking forward to leaving the school. The older boys in year 11 are being particularly difficult. They are causing a lot of problems while waiting for the bus, such as obstructing the pavement instead of remaining in the playground.

Your strategy

When a duty is done by more than one person, inconsistencies may occur. Large, boisterous year 11 boys can be intimidating and the easy option in this kind of situation is to let them do as they like rather than try to deal with the problem and get involved in a conflict.

The easy option is to report it to the headteacher who can then have a serious talk to all the students travelling by bus. The staff could meet and discuss their strategies and agree one they will all be prepared to enforce.

However, if the problem is to be dealt with when it occurs and you feel confident enough to try, then you should go for the non-conflict approach. Shouting and bullish tactics may work, and a tough teacher can certainly get the boys to move back inside the gate, but many teachers are not able to do this, or feel uncomfortable doing it in this way.

Avoid conflict

The easiest method is to be friendly and assertive. Persist with your request when the student does not move. For example, pick the ones who you think are most likely to respond, smile and get talking to them:

T   Excuse me, lads. Will you wait for the bus inside the gate please, because you are blocking the pavement and other people cannot pass.

Then go to the next group and do the same. If the first group haven't moved you will need to be more persuasive and insistent:

T   Come on, Peter, when people want to pass they have to cross over because they are too frightened to ask you to move. I know you don't mean to scare them, you're all right. So move back into the playground then you won't be in their way.

This method is based upon reason and enables the student to recognise that his actions have consequences. In this case it is intimidating passers-by which is probably not intentional, nor his desire.

Taking the matter further

Some students may continue to stand their ground, even after several polite requests, so find out their names and take no further action then. Report the incident to the head or deputy and let them deal with it. It is not worth getting into a conflict situation where you may lose. They have probably got used to standing on the pavement because other teachers may not have been able to get them to move, so one more day will not make much difference.

The avoidance of any conflict may work, but if it doesn't you do not lose any of your authority as a teacher back in the classroom.

After-school fights

All through lunch and into the afternoon you have been increasingly aware of the tense atmosphere in the school. Something is afoot, and whatever it is, it has spread like wildfire from the oldest to the youngest students. Just before break something happens that confirms your suspicions that there will be a fight after school, and it seems that a small group in your class may be the ringleaders.

Your strategy

When the whole school is buzzing, the other teachers will probably have drawn the same conclusions as you. You all need to agree on what should be done, so it is important that you share your hunch with your colleagues, and then report it to the head if it looks serious.

Events that are supposed to be kept secret from the teachers can be dealt with in a number of ways. If you just want to stop them and are not interested in finding out who is involved, you should let the students know that you are aware that trouble is brewing. Then be at the most likely venues as the home bell sounds, so that the staff presence will deter anyone from going ahead with their plans. The problem with this is that it may only postpone the event, feuds between individuals or other schools do not go away, they recur.

Resolving the problem

You could question one or two students who you know will not be involved or interested, but will know what is going to happen. Talk to them individually and be friendly so as to re-assure them. Once you have the names of the students involved you can ease up, but if they do not co-operate get a little heavier by letting them know that with-holding information will get them into trouble. Then offer them a way out by asking them to write down the names and give them to you anonymously. The next course of action depends upon the circumstances. Some favour intercepting the boys before the end of school. This should be done with one of the senior managers. The obvious difficulty will be that the students can deny the allegations because nothing has happened. Clever questioning may draw out the story and then you can put a case together by using other information and any previous 'form'. The students have to find a way of resolving the problem before it ends in violence. This is a difficult path through the situation and will only be successful if the staff involved are experienced, and even then the students may not co-operate.

Letting it happen

Alternatively, let the situation develop a bit more before taking any action. Arrange for staff to be in positions outside the gate where they can be inconspicuous. When the 'spectators' begin to arrive, all the attention will be on the students. Once the incident begins, move in and intercept the key individuals. If you are too slow the crowd will disperse and the boys who were fighting will literally melt away, but you will have seen them and there will be witnesses to help back up the case.

Involve parents

Schools have their own ways of dealing with students caught fighting, and one effective method is to interview them with their parents. This formalises the incident and enables the parents to get the full story and discuss the sanctions with the Head. The result may be a temporary exclusion. This indicates to the students as well as the parents that fighting will not be tolerated. When the excluded student returns there should be a period where they are helped to modify their behaviour and repair the situation.

Students being abusive to teachers outside school

> The walk home from school is a very pleasant one and during the summer months you look forward to it. The lighter evenings bring out the youngsters and they often play in the streets. On one occasion a student from your school calls out something abusive as you pass by.

Your strategy

Hopefully, this will not happen to you but if it does you should not respond in any way at the time. Generally, if students see their teacher they will either be embarrassed and not acknowledge you unless you say something to them first, or they will be pleased to see you and say 'hello'. Sometimes they may say it in a cheeky way because they are shy, but they do not mean to be rude. Quite the opposite, they will be trying to get your attention because they like you. The abusive comments will come from students who are feeling resentful because of something you said or did to them at school. That is why it is very important to repair and rebuild your relationship with a student after you have had to have words about his or her behaviour.

Your approach

The abusive comment is a form of challenge. The student uses the neutral ground of the streets to 'take a pop' at you because he or she feels that your authority does not extend beyond the school. When something like this happens, get a good look at the student so you can identify him or her later, then walk on. Do not slow down, or speed up, and do not look back.

Next day, find out the name of the student and report the incident to someone more senior, then send a message to the form teacher explaining what happened. Ask for the student to be sent to you.

The student will probably know why he or she has been called and may be feeling very sheepish. Invite the student in and direct him or her to a seat. Sit down and spend about half a minute arranging your papers. When you are ready, tell the student why he or she has been sent for. Explain how his or her comments were disrespectful and that everyone has the right to walk down the street free of harassment. You may feel that the parents should also be present at the meeting so they are aware of the student's behaviour. Make it clear that rudeness to teachers cannot be tolerated. Modulate your comments according to students' age and the amount of humility they show. The arrogant ones may only respond to very assertive and quite clever comments. You may wish to place a report of the incident in the student's file and let his or her parents know you are doing it. Suggest that a report will be drafted but not put on file immediately.

Choosing the consequences

Offer the student a chance to repair the situation by behaving appropriately. This should be specified and could include opening doors for people, offering to help teachers, and volunteering when things need to be done. Set a time period of a week or two, and if he or she adheres to the scheme, the report will remain in your desk. Praise the student when he or she does what you ask and say that if he or she keeps it up you will write and let his or her parents know how well he or she is doing.

This opportunity of redemption will prevent any negative feelings and allow you a chance to rebuild your relationship with the student.

Summary

The problems that occur outside the classroom will be harder to deal with, because we do not have the same kind of authority as we do inside the classroom. In the lesson we are in charge and whatever we decide should happen invariably will. Students may try to challenge us but they do it in our domain. The situation changes out in the playground. It is still part of the school and we are still the teachers, but it is their space and they have far more freedom to do what they like, how they like. Beyond the school gate, we all become equal members of the same society and students may question a teacher's jurisdiction outside the school. We need to adopt different methods and ways of addressing the students if we are to succeed in helping them develop the right kinds of behaviour.

Key points for managing behaviour outside the classroom and beyond the school gates

- When you have to move classes, brief students on how you want them to behave prior to leaving the room.
- Match consequences to the broken rules, for example, when a student defaces a display get them to help look after a notice-board.
- Try getting the victim to confront the bully and explain how the harassment makes them feel.
- When you catch bullies get them to write a report explaining what they were doing to show up inconsistencies between them, and provide written evidence for further action.
- Separate students involved in disputes during playground games so they can cool off. When disputes are not serious, restart the game and get them back into it quickly.
- Avoid public showdowns with students, go for the non-conflict approach but make sure everyone involved and those looking on

know that there are consequences when rules are broken, and you will always follow things up later.

- Ignore cheeky comments and persist with your request.
- Deal with after-school fights collectively with your colleagues and make sure you know the procedures.
- Never respond to abusive comments made by students out of school. Deal with them the next day in school.

5

DEALING WITH DISTRACTIONS

Introduction

A teacher's life is punctuated by a chain of distractions, disturbances and interruptions that break up the class-based activities. For most of the time they are blanked out but occasionally the problem becomes too intrusive and some kind of action must be taken. The skill is in how the teacher responds so that the students' concentration is maintained, and the lesson allowed to continue.

There are all sorts of distractions, some are unavoidable and some are not. The ones that come from within the classroom are usually related to behaviour. A student may make a silly sound, or break wind, which could cause a severe disruption. Someone may turn up to the lesson late and enter the room in a heroic way, creating a lot of noise and comments. A student may even possess a mobile phone which starts to ring while you are talking. All of these need to be handled with care and speed if their effects are not going to interrupt the learning. They are behavioural issues and can be managed in similar ways to many of the problems described elsewhere in this book. The emphasis should always be on pre-empting problems, but when they do occur a graduated response that avoids conflict is best.

Distractions may come from beyond the classroom walls and require different methods to deal with them effectively. These are not discipline issues and the students are not to blame for them, but you will have to get them to co-operate and behave in particular ways if the distractions are to be overcome.

This chapter deals with these kinds of issues and offers useful strategies for dealing with them in ways that will cause the minimum of fuss and disturbance. The emphasis is on prevention, and offering choices when resolving the problems with the students.

Breaking wind during the lesson

> You have been working hard with the class to improve their powers of concentration. One of your successes is their writing. They have been working silently for ten minutes and you are very pleased with their progress. Suddenly the silence is broken and one of the boys passes wind very loudly so everyone can hear.

Your strategy

Boys can be quite crude at times and events like this are extremely hard to avoid. When they happen they cannot be ignored. They usually prompt a wave of laughter and pretended asphyxiation. There is little chance of it going unnoticed by the rest of the class who will take it as an opportunity to go off-task.

Preventing this problem is very difficult. It is not easy to raise the issue in a serious discussion and you can hardly put *Passing wind should not be done during the lessons* in the student handbook or the school rules. There are some preventative measures you can try. Politeness is one of the social skills students can be taught. This could be done during discussions about the kind of behaviour that is acceptable in your classroom. Unsociable behaviour could include sudden outbursts, silly noises, humming, tapping and clicking sounds. Belching and passing wind may also be included, and might provoke a few giggles but you have made your point. Hopefully the distractions during the discussions about behaviour will not be as bad as the interruptions that could occur if a student made one of these noises in your lesson.

Your approach

Older boys will pass wind loudly to gain attention and deliberately disturb the class. The response of the other students will be difficult to control because they will often go on about the smell and will object to sitting near to the person who produced it. When you have no doubt who did it you should send him out of the room to the school exclusion zone. He will have to negotiate his return to the class with you and agree to observe the behaviour code. Try to make his exit a quick, unobtrusive one:

T Alan, that was very rude. Pack up your things and go to the zone for the rest of the lesson please.

S But Sir, I couldn't help it.

T Maybe you couldn't, but we shall discuss that at the end of the lesson. Now go, and I will come and see you when the bell goes.

Be clear and assertive. Do not enter into any discussion or argument. This action will probably satisfy the other students so you can continue with the lesson. You may not wish to take it this far, if not simply tell the student you will want to see him after the lesson. Make it a short, sharp, request then resume what you were doing.

Sometimes you will not be able to tell who the culprit is so your response should be minimal. Open the windows, tell the students who are overacting and being melodramatic to sit down, and then continue with your lesson.

Calm your class down

If the students cannot be sensible and quieten down you could try a short period of note-taking. There is nothing like copying a few notes down off the board to get the class back under control:

S Phew! What a stink, etc ...

T I'll open some windows.

S You pig ..., that was evil!

T Right, this seems to be a good time to make some notes of the key points. Copy them off the board please.

It should only take about five minutes. Then if some students persist you can address them individually.

T These notes must be copied down. Either you stop disturbing others or you go to the zone. Then you will have to copy them up for homework.

The students can choose and in most cases they will get on with the work and cut out the chit-chat.

Try humour

Humour is a very effective means of taking the heat out of the situation. The students who are overacting are not really suffocating so you could play along with the gag by making a humorous remark like:

> 'It's windy today!'
> 'Someone over-did the beans at lunchtime!'
> 'We really must have a word with cook about the dinners!'
> 'Whoever did that is in need of dietary advice!'

Comments like these will put an end to the play acting and give rise to general laughter which can then be allowed to die down. Then you can get the class under control more easily because they will not find your quips as stimulating as the show of amateur dramatics.

Arriving late to your lesson

A student arrives late and the lesson has already begun. You have introduced the topic and are discussing a worksheet you have circulated. How do you deal with the interruption?

Your strategy

Students arrive late for all sorts of reasons. Some are legitimate, and some are not. They can be very disruptive and waste valuable time. There are many ways of dealing with interruptions depending on when they occur in the day. Schools usually start the day with a registration period, so many of the latenesses caused by morning transport problems can be absorbed in this time and not affect the lessons. Students are expected to be on time for all their lessons which may be a little difficult if they have to come from a room at the other end of the school and there is no time between periods.

Some teachers usually make allowances for this and do not start their lessons immediately. They deal with routine matters in this time such as checking homework, organizing desks and giving out resources. It is also an opportunity to have a friendly word with students and get to know them better. You should make it clear to everyone in the class that the lesson will start at the same time each week and insist that they are in the room and seated by that time.

Your approach 1

Being prepared is the best strategy. Try and decide how you will incorporate latecomers into the class if you are likely to get them regularly. Most students have their places in the room. Either you have allocated them, or they have chosen to sit in the same place on a regular basis. A late arrival will interrupt the flow of the lesson if they have to go across the room to reach their seat. To avoid this you could leave one or two places empty near the door for latecomers if you have enough spare seats available. When they arrive you direct them to the empty places as unobtrusively as possible:

S   Sorry I'm late, Miss.
T   Good morning, Jane, if you could sit there for the time being (pointing to the seat near the door) and will you see me at the end of the lesson, please? We are just starting to look at how glaciers have changed the landscape. (Handing her a worksheet.)

The teacher does not attempt to find out why the student is late because the rest of the class is waiting for the lesson to resume. A simple greeting followed by a direction and a request to see her later are all that is required. She can find out the reason for the lateness after the lesson and take action then if necessary.

Sometimes we judge students too quickly, especially if they have built up a reputation in the past. Assumptions like these can be dangerous, especially if you are going to put off finding out why a student is late until the end of the lesson. There is always the temptation to treat the student as if she is in the wrong during the lesson and it may be unjust. It is better to assume that the students have legitimate reasons for their lateness and welcome them into the class, then forget about it until the end.

Your approach 2

There are some teachers who like to deal with the students immediately if they are habitually late. This is disruptive and can be embarrassing. A colleague challenged a student in this way with devastating results:

T   Oh hello, Carol (he said sarcastically), it is nice of you to join us. What time do you call this?

S   I'm sorry, Mr Brown, but ...

T   You are twenty five minutes late and this is not the first time.

S   Sorry but ... (tears are beginning to show in her eyes).

T   Well! What's your excuse then?

S   I had to ... (she stops when another student enters).

T   Another one dropping in for a visit, and why are you late, Jane?

S   I am very sorry, Sir. I was with Carol. Her father was rushed to the hospital with a heart attack and I went with her.

The silence said it all. The teacher was quite sick with the way he had handled it. He had assumed she was late for the usual reasons and questioned her unnecessarily in front of the class.

Your approach 3

Some students use lateness as a means of getting attention and cause a great deal of disruption. They need skillful handling to avoid letting them succeed. Bobby was in year 10 and was not considered to be particularly outstanding academically and he did not shine at sport. In fact he was below average at everything he did in school. He had been going through a period of silly behaviour and many of his teachers had put it down to a need to be noticed. He steered clear of anything that required competing against his peers. The kinds of things he did were often destructive and he would even bully younger children. He began arriving late for lessons so he could be the last to enter the room. He would wait till the lesson had started and then burst in and stand by the door. The teacher would stop talking and Bobby would apologise with an excuse like he had forgotten his bag and had to go back and get it. The teacher would usually accept his apology and tell him to sit down. He would swagger across the class-room kicking bags as he went and then sit down in a very loud way. The teacher would resume the lesson and then be interrupted by Bobby opening the Velcro flap of his bag rather noisily. Eventually he settled and behaved sensibly for the rest of the lesson.

The teacher could have insisted he sat at the spare place by the door to avoid the fuss he caused as he made his way to his usual seat. The trick is to avoid over-servicing attention-seeking behaviour that is disruptive, but to make a point of rewarding the student when they do something right. You may also need to talk to the student about his behaviour and explain that arriving late and causing a lot of fuss is not acceptable. Agree some targets together and make sure they are rewarded when the student meets them.

Your approach 4

Lateness in colleges is a problem because there is a different approach to discipline. The students are expected to take responsibility for their own actions. Judging journey times to college is often poorly done by some students, resulting in regular lateness. A solution to this is to give out the most important notes, teach the key points and issue the notices in the first fifteen minutes. Late students then have to make up the work in their own time. They will quickly learn that they have a choice. Being punctual avoids missing important work, and they will probably understand the lesson better, but if they choose to have a lie-in they know what the consequence will be.

Mobile phones in the classroom

A group are admiring a student's mobile phone when you enter the classroom. How can you avoid having to deal with an interruption to your lesson caused by one of their phones ringing?

Your strategy

Mobile phones are becoming popular status symbols for young people and the age of the owners is getting lower. They are bringing them into school and causing all sorts of problems to do with security, as well as disturbing lessons. A school where a lot of students own them will need a rule insisting that mobile phones are either switched off during lessons or left at home.

Owners of mobile phones like to show them off and will place them on the desk at the start of a lesson so they can be seen. You may feel the rule should extend to them being kept in bags during the lessons as well. Students who forget to switch off their phones should expect to have them confiscated if they ring.

A rule like this is harder to enforce in a college. Students lead more complicated lives than schoolchildren and will argue that a mobile phone is essential. The responsibility of enforcing the rule falls almost solely on the teacher, so it is worth discussing mobile phones when you are establishing a classroom code. Then the students will be clear about what is expected and what the consequences will be if they do not co-operate. Confiscation would not be a very successful option with adult students but something is required because there will be times when they forget the rule.

Reminding about the rules

To avoid any conflict, remind the students of the rule about mobile phones at the start of each lesson:

T   Now, I would like you all to check that your mobile phones are switched off and put away in your bags. Thank you.

A permanent note in the register is a useful reminder to prevent you from forgetting to do this.

When students leave their phones switched on and get a call you should insist that they switch off rather than answer. The class cannot possibly wait while one student has a telephone conversation, no matter how brief it is. For example:

T Will you switch it off please and then either put it in your bag or on my desk.

Giving them a choice will let them own their behaviour. A student will almost certainly want to put it in their bag rather than part with it. They may want to find out who called but you must insist that the phone is put away to avoid any further interruptions.

I have seen students get up and go outside the room to take a call during practical lessons. It may be less disruptive to let them do so and then talk to them when they return.

When you do have to confiscate a phone, do not make a big deal over it. Then when you return it, begin with a comment about the phone to repair the relationship:

T Nice mobile, I bet it is useful. I am thinking of getting one. There is a time and a place for their use and my lesson is not one of them. I found it very annoying when your phone rang because it disturbed everyone in the class and prevented them from giving me their full attention.

S Sorry Mr Wright.

T I want you to promise to remember to switch it off during lessons in future.

Give them their phone, smile and let them go.

A wasp flies into the classroom

It is a warm, sunny, September day at the start of the term. The students are working well when suddenly a wasp flies in. Someone lets out a scream causing several others to start swiping the air with their books in an effort to swat it.

Your strategy

September is the worst time of the year for wasps. A long, balmy August followed by a warm September provides ideal conditions for wasps to flourish. People will instinctively swipe at a wasp the moment it comes near them. On occasions the wasp will sting someone, especially if it gets trapped under clothing against bare skin. Stings can range from being very uncomfortable to extremely painful. In extreme cases they can bring on *anaphylactic shock* in some people which may lead to death. So you have a duty to do something. You cannot tell the class to ignore it (because they won't) and hope it will go away. You may be frightened by wasps yourself and want it out of your room, so action is required.

Find a magazine or newspaper and roll it up. Wait for the wasp to settle and then swat it. If you cannot do it yourself, ask one of the students to do it for you or send someone to fetch a colleague. The whole thing will be very distracting so do not expect to resume the lesson until the wasp is eliminated. An alternative strategy may be to open up all the windows and doors and then try to 'shoo' it out.

Important visitors arrive at your lesson unannounced

The class has just started a new piece of work and students are in pairs discussing it. They are enthusiastic and their conversations are quite animated and loud. Suddenly the headteacher enters the room accompanied by one of the governors and a visitor from the local feeder school.

Your strategy

The visitors may want to do one of several things. They may be on a guided tour of the school so you only need to greet them and then resume what you were doing. Or they may ask what is going on, and will usually only have time for a quick explanation. A useful discipline is to encapsulate the primary aim or purpose of the lesson into one sentence. You can use this to start the lesson off so the students will know why they are doing the activity. The reply you give to the visitors can be this summary of the aims. Give them the lesson plan to look over then explain why the students are working in groups in the way they are. The following phrases may be useful:

> 'The students really get a lot out of discussion work.'
> 'Group discussions allow them to exchange ideas and consider alternative options.'
> 'Some of these students really excel when they have to justify their point of view.'
> 'I find that discussion work enables students who do not express themselves well on paper to participate and show they have something to offer.'

Never apologise for the level of noise. If you believe it is acceptable as part of the activity, then you do not have to give excuses for it. The most important factor is whether you can bring the class to your attention and quieten them without having to shout. As long as you are not disturbing the classes nearby and the noise does not prevent the students from hearing each other, you have nothing to worry about.

Summary

Many distractions in schools are unavoidable and teachers need to be able to work around them by thinking, and acting, quickly. Sometimes things happen that cut across the smooth delivery of the lesson and result in everyone becoming distracted. At other times the interruption has a rippling effect and can be contained at source. Many of the distractions can be pre-empted and a plan devised to overcome them quickly. This chapter deals with a variety of incidents that may occur, and offers some strategies and approaches for resolving them in ways that minimize their effects.

Key points for dealing with distractions

- Humour is a good way of dealing with an embarrassing incident by taking the heat out of it.
- Latecomers should be invited into the lesson and dealt with at the end.
- Students should be reminded to switch off mobile phones and pagers during lessons.
- Insects can be dangerous as well as a nuisance and need to be removed from a room where there are students.
- Always greet visitors when they enter your room and offer them a short explanation of the lesson and a copy of the lesson plan.

6

RELATIONSHIPS WITH COLLEAGUES AND STUDENTS

Introduction

Teaching is a profession with its own codes and conventions. Members have a responsibility to uphold the codes of behaviour and act in a way that will not bring the profession into disrepute. We are all equal as colleagues, irrespective of individual status within our own institution, and everyone has a right to be treated in a professional way.

On occasions the codes get forgotten and problems occur and at these times we look to each other for support. There are many opportunities for co-operation, and much of what we do as teachers is done in small groups and teams. Whatever the situation, there will always be times when we shall want to call on others for advice, assistance, resources or just someone to listen to our problems. Cultivating and nurturing good working relationships should be one of our aims. Getting along with each other will make the job easier and more enjoyable. There will be times when you find you cannot agree with a view expressed by one of your colleagues. When that happens, accept that everyone has their own opinions and agree to differ so that it will not interfere with your view of them as a person.

Senior colleagues have a wealth of experience to offer, but they are not perfect. People do make mistakes and these can be infuriating at times but we should deal with their errors professionally. No one likes being criticised, least of all by a junior colleague. Equally, no one enjoys being a victim of someone else's unprofessional conduct. Getting the balance right by knowing when to speak out and when to remain silent is a skill learned over time. If a colleague does act in an unprofessional way you should evaluate the situation and decide whether it really effects you so much to want to pursue it further. Minor things are probably best left alone and if they occur again a gentle word is all that will be required. More serious incidents that eat away at you and hinder your performance are worth pursuing so that you can put your mind at rest. The worry some teachers have is knowing how to deal with a problem when it involves someone more senior.

This chapter takes up some of these issues and looks at ways of resolving them that avoid conflict. In particular, criticism from a colleague, noise from the class next door, students complaining about another teacher to you and the common problem of double-booking of rooms and resources. There are also strategies for dealing with a classroom assistant who contradicts you and students who need to leave your lessons for extra-curricular activities and sports events.

The second part of the chapter covers the relationships teachers have with their classes. The role of teachers is to educate the students and this involves maintaining the authority that is conferred on them by virtue of their status. If their status is undermined their authority is at risk. Teachers work hard at their classroom management skills, but do not have the same degree of control over other things their students say or do outside of the lesson. We need to be aware of these and the pitfalls that can occur between staff and students so that we can avoid becoming trapped by them. For example, discovering you have a nickname you do not like, students with crushes on you, finding yourself alone in a room with a student of the opposite sex, and dealing with the Christmas mistletoe! Sensitive and intelligent handling of each of these cases is essential if you are to maintain a good rapport with your students. The emphasis throughout this chapter is on adopting a considered approach and remaining calm to avoid unnecessary conflict.

A colleague criticises you in front of your class

The school has a specialist music teacher on the staff. He takes each class from reception to year 6 for a thirty minute session each week. The form teacher recently joined the school and was told to take her class along to the music room at the allotted time. She was unclear of her role so she stayed for the lesson. After a few weeks she began to feel that her presence was not really necessary and her time could be better used.

At the start of the second term she went to the music room with her class, sat quietly at the back and marked books. The children were being taught to keep a rhythm by singing a simple song, but when the teacher tried to get them to sing it as a round they got confused. The teacher got frustrated but persisted even when it was clear it was not going to work. Suddenly he stopped the class and addressed the form teacher.

> 'Perhaps if your teacher stopped marking books and joined in we would be able to do this right.'

She was shocked and it showed in her expression. She replied:

> 'I asked Mrs O'Connor (a senior teacher) what we were supposed to do and she said she marked books while you took the class.'

The music teacher looked angry as he spoke:

> 'Some teachers mark books, but they are not supposed to you know. They are supposed to join in with the children so they can learn how to teach music.'

This conversation took place in the lesson time in front of the children who were listening and taking it all in. Some even began to make comments to each other. The form teacher closed her books and joined the activity but was clearly not very happy. The music teacher kept going with the round but it still did not go right. When the class had left the room the form teacher went over to the music teacher and said:

> 'I would like to talk to you at break, will you be in this room?'

Your strategy

Whatever the reason may be, criticism of another teacher in front of students is unprofessional. It gives the impression that the staff are not working together as a team, and provides a 'chink' for students to exploit. Form teachers put in a great deal of effort to build up good relationships with their classes so that order is achieved and effective learning can take place. When the teacher was criticised in front of the class, her authority was undermined.

Situation 1

The conversation she has at the meeting will be her opportunity to explain to the music teacher (MT) how he had misjudged the situation. It was caused by his belief that he could act in a bullish way and get away with it. The form teacher's response followed these lines:

FT I wanted to talk to you about the way you treated me this morning.

MT Yes, I could see you were upset but really I didn't mean to single you out because other teachers have been doing the same thing and it's not on.

He is shifting the emphasis to himself and when this occurs he needs to be brought back to the main issue because the meeting was not called so he could give his excuses.

FT That is a separate issue. The point I want to make is that you acted unprofessionally by criticising me in front of my class which is unforgivable.

She clarifies the issues and stresses the one she wishes to pursue. Her reference to professionalism focuses the discussion on the seriousness of the incident. No one likes to be accused of unprofessional behaviour but in this particular case it has to be highlighted.

MT Well I hope I can be forgiven and that we can still have a working relationship for the sake of the children.

This is a clever move because he is using the teacher's apparent inability to forgive to show that the students will be the ones to suffer. The onus is on her and if she makes the wrong decision it will be her fault. Let us not forget that it was his initial behaviour that led to this. She moves him back to his actions:

FT Maybe I shall be able to rebuild our professional relationship (notice this is not about forgiveness) because I am a professional (in contrast to him) and agree that the children should not suffer but at the moment I feel you behaved outrageously. I have never had anyone speak to me like that in all of the fifteen years I have been teaching.

The teacher finished expressing her feelings. The music teacher is quite taken aback and hopefully he realises where he went wrong. If he does not, then he certainly knows he cannot bully this teacher and needs to think before he speaks to her in the future.

The form teacher did not go out of her way to cause conflict but she was not prepared to be treated in this way by a colleague of equal status. It may be harder to deal with someone more senior but if they are allowed to treat others in this way and get away with it, it will just continue.

Situation 2

Approaching a senior colleague, such as a head of department (HOD), should be done with care. Make an appointment and if they ask you what the meeting will be about, tell them that it is a personal matter. On the day of the meeting try to be calm. Once in their room ask if they could redirect any telephone calls because what you have to say is going to be difficult for you and you would appreciate it if there were no interruptions.

Begin what you have to say in a positive way. For example:

T   Thank you for sparing the time to see me. I know you are very busy but I feel that it is important that I talk to you.

Try to be friendly and not get aggressive even if you are still very aggrieved by what he said to you.

HOD Now, how can I help you?

T   Well I was very taken aback by the way you spoke to me the other day and after careful thought, I decided it would be best to see you and discuss it rather than let it go and end up harbouring bad thoughts.

What you are telling him is that there is a problem and it cannot be pushed under the carpet.

T   You criticized my performance as a teacher in front of my class which undermined my authority and compromised my position. You may have a valid reason and I shall be happy to discuss it at another time but that is a separate issue. I felt that you did not have any respect for me as a person which is saddening considering we are colleagues. I expect to be treated politely and courteously by my colleagues, in the same way as I do to them.

HOD I am very sorry. I assure you I was not trying to put you down and I had no idea you felt this way.

T   That is why we needed to discuss it. If you have a problem with my work you need to come out and say it. I am not a mind-reader. But there is a time and a place! As far as I am concerned I am trying to do my best and do not deserve to be treated in this way.

You may succeed in gaining an apology from the head of department but be wary. She may begrudge giving it and try to take it away. You have said that you want to be told when you do not do something satisfactorily, but at the right time. You have also pointed out that you do not deserve this treatment. However, the HOD may feel that she wants to 'win' something as well.

HOD I take your point. I shall ensure it never happens again and I am sorry for the way I spoke to you. However, I do think you should be more careful with ... (She is interrupted).

T I appreciate your apology and I welcome the opportunity to discuss how I can improve, but not today thank you. I would like more time to get over this incident. I do hope you understand.

HOD Yes, of course.

T ... and that you can see why I needed this meeting so that we could rebuild our professional relationship.

HOD Of course yes, and once again I am sorry. Just let me know when you are ready and we can meet again.

Stay in control

It was necessary to interrupt the HOD when she started talking about what you did wrong to enable you to keep control, because it is your meeting. Your interruption should begin with an offer of thanks which is a less aggressive way than saying you do not want to talk about the issue of your performance. You need to control the direction of the conversation so you postpone further criticism, as well as giving your ego some time to heal. The HOD may be understanding and will agree with you. By the end, she is aware of your feelings and is leaving the decision to you. You will have made your point in a non-threatening way by assertively controlling what is and is not discussed. The meeting will let the HOD know there is a problem and if she is reasonable she will find ways of solving it. If she is not, there is little more you can do without causing unnecessary friction and possibly making things difficult for yourself in the future.

A noisy class disrupts your lesson

For most of the time, the classes going on in the rooms near yours are fairly quiet. There is an exception when one class regularly disrupts your lesson at the same time every week. The noise disturbs your students and prevents them from concentrating. You have put up with it for several weeks because you thought it would eventually stop. It actually seems to be getting worse.

Relationships with colleagues and students

Your strategy

Do not do anything during the lesson. You have put up with it until now so one more lesson will not make much difference. The students may find the noise distracting but they will work through it if you give them tasks that do not require quiet conditions. You may need to change your lesson plan to allow for this. Group discussion is ideal because their own conversations will drown the background noise. Whatever you choose to do will only have to last for the lesson because you will deal with the problem before the next one.

Your approach 1

After the lesson, find out from the school timetable which member of staff was taking the class that was making the noise. Then arrange to see him at the first convenient time. Begin by checking the facts:

You   Bob, did you have a class in Room B1 for Period 3?

Bob   Yes, that was year 9 English. Why?

You   What were you doing in there? I could hear it next door! (Said in a smiling, jovial way.)

Bob   We have been improvising scenes from Shakespeare. I got the kids to imagine they were Romeo or Juliet, but in modern times. They acted out their own lover's tiff. I'm terribly sorry I didn't think about you next door. I hope I haven't caused you too much trouble.

You   No, no, you're all right, Bob. It sounds really interesting. I bet the kids loved. it. I know you didn't mean it but the walls are so thin that we can follow nearly every detail. My class were beginning to become disruptive because they couldn't concentrate. How much longer will you be doing that kind of activity?

Avoid conflict

The conversation remains fairly light-hearted and the teacher gets an opportunity to explain which prevents you jumping to the wrong conclusion. He realises that his lesson has disturbed others and is given a chance to apologize. You can accept his apology gracefully and a compliment about his lesson helps smooth the situation. This is reached by gently inquiring whether he plans any future lessons of this type.

Bob Well I was planning two more lessons of rehearsal. I shall organise the class differently so they do not all do their bits at once. That's why it was so noisy, they were all going at it together. I shall get them to rehearse for homework and do their performances next week. It will be quieter, I promise.

You Cheers, Bob.

Everyone is happy and the problem is solved without any acrimony. It might have led to a breakdown in staff relationships if it had been handled differently.

Your approach 2

The problem may have been harder to resolve if the teacher was having difficulties managing his class. Let us suppose that Bob is having trouble keeping his class quiet, and the din occurs again during the next lesson. You may want to try a different approach.

You I am sorry to bring this up again, Bob, but the noise from your room is still as loud and it is disturbing my class. You said you would try something different with them. Are you all right with them or are they a bit of a handful? I know Steve and Laura can be a bit over the top and mouthy at times.

You need to be more sensitive as it would seem that the other teacher cannot keep his class as quiet as it should be. It is useful for the teacher to hear that others have problems with that class, because it shows they are not isolated and perhaps even beginning to feel they cannot cope. Putting it this way prevents it from sounding like you are judging his skills as a teacher. When you want to discuss a sensitive issue like classroom management you should try to be open, and convey the message that no one is perfect and you have probably experienced similar problems. Then there will be more chance of an open dialogue developing and with discussion comes solutions.

Taking the matter further

The problem of the noise may still continue, and so you will have to resort to further action. Talk it over in confidence with your head of department and stress that you do need something to be done because it is having an adverse effect on your lessons. The other teacher needs help, and a good head of department will be able to give him some strategies to try. Alternatively, talk to his head of department directly, but remember to do it diplomatically as this is a delicate matter that could damage a teacher's reputation.

The easy option is to do nothing and hope the problem goes away, but until it does, you and your students will have to suffer. Leaving the matter does not help the other teacher because he needs the support and guidance of someone with experience so his students can learn the right way to behave in lessons.

A colleague enters your class and complains about the noise

Your lesson is proceeding really well. The introduction and exposition of the topic was short and punchy and got the whole class interested and raring to go. The room is bubbling with industrious activity as the students embark on the investigative task with zeal. Moving from one group to another you know you have cracked it and they are all learning. Suddenly the door opens and another teacher enters. She looks around the room but does not seem to see you because you are sitting with one of the groups. She enquires loudly, 'What is the meaning of this noise? My class is trying to work next door.'

A colleague enters your class and complains about the noise

Your strategy

The walls of some schools do not stop sounds from travelling very well. Loud classes and noisy activities can interfere with the lessons taking place in nearby rooms. When this becomes a problem teachers need to co-operate with each other and work together. They must keep their own class under control so that the noise level is not intrusive. At the same time, they should also be understanding and tolerant of occasional increases in noise that occur in adjacent rooms.

There will be occasions when you want to do something that may be noisier than usual, like showing a video, singing or doing a practical technology activity. Plan carefully and take the problem of noise into consideration. Then inform the teachers in the rooms nearby of what you will be doing. Explain that there may be some unavoidable noise and apologise in advance for any inconvenience it may cause. You could ask them if they have any suggestions to help you reduce the noise. Consider moving rooms for excessively loud lessons like singing or drama. More open spaces may be better locations. In this way everyone is made aware of your lesson and what to expect and the problem of the noise is shared.

Your approach

It is inexcusable for a teacher to burst into your room and address the class without first establishing whether you are around. Teachers have an agreed protocol to ensure that their professional integrity and authority is maintained. She may have had a very good reason for coming to your room but that does not give her the right to assume authority in it. Do not deal with the issue of interrupting your lesson, apologize, and defer it by arranging to meet with her later:

You I am sorry for the disturbance my class caused earlier. I shall make sure they are quieter in future.

T That's okay, they were fine after I came in.

You I wanted to talk to you about that. I felt undermined when you came in and spoke to my students without asking me. I wouldn't dream of doing that to you.

T Yes, I am sorry about that. I didn't see you, and thought the class was unattended and running riot.

Be careful now, do not respond to her last comment no matter how annoyed you are because you will be drawn into an unnecessary discussion about what is acceptable practice. Accept the spirit of what she is saying.

You Thank you. I accept your apology. It was an easy mistake to make because you probably couldn't see me right over at the back of the room and sitting down with a group of students. But in future, can you speak to me before you talk to my class so that I retain my authority with them?

This approach offers a way out for the other teacher and clarifies with her what you would like to happen in the future.

Avoid conflict

The teacher who entered your room made an error. She could have avoided any conflict if she had enquired where you were instead of assuming the class was unattended:

T Robert, where is your teacher?

S Over there, Miss.

T Thank you.

She should then ask to speak to you outside in the corridor. That way she avoids being critical or commenting on your classroom management skills in front of your students. The matter should be resolved promptly because your students need you. Apologize and reassure your colleague that you will try to reduce the level of noise for the remainder of the lesson. When you go back to your room, go round to each group and ask the students to be quieter because other classes are complaining. Do not make an announcement to the whole group because it will stop the discussions, which may be a shame if they have been going well.

Removing students from lessons

A similar kind of problem may occur with students who have learning difficulties and need to be taken out of lessons for things like reading and spelling tests. When the teacher comes to get them, she should knock, enter quietly and wait till you are free. She may want students to go with her so she should ask. She may be in the habit of putting her head round the door and calling the students without even acknowledging you. You should see her later and explain that they are your students during that lesson and you would appreciate it if she asked for your permission to let them go. Of course you will accept, but to ask is a common courtesy, and polite behaviour is a requirement in the teaching profession.

Students complain to you about another teacher

A number of students in your form group ask to talk to you about an important matter. They appear fed up and clearly have a grievance they want to air. When asked what it is, they name one of your colleagues and begin to complain about him.

Your strategy

Do not get involved. The moment students start to talk about one of your colleagues, stop them and tell them that it would be unprofessional of you to hear what they have to say. Students may dislike a teacher or the way he teaches. They may even have a legitimate complaint but you are not the person who deals with it and you should make that clear to them. Some schools and colleges have a complaints procedure for dealing with assessment problems and that may be the channel they should use. When there is no formal procedure they must decide for themselves what to do. Other teachers should not get involved.

There is a great temptation to feel flattered that they have chosen to confide in you. It makes you feel you are doing things right and the other teacher is doing things wrong. This may not be the case so do not read it as a compliment.

Some teachers need to be liked by their students more than others, and their lack of experience results in their inability to separate the friendly contact from this kind of situation. You may feel good, but have misread the signs. They may have confided in you because they think the form teacher is the person to tell.

The best course of action is to briefly explain why you cannot get involved, and then send them off. They may not be happy with your decision but in the longer term you will have acted professionally. Do not give any advice on what they should do and do not appear too sympathetic, just be civil and polite. The older, more mature students may take their problem up with the teacher themselves. That is the best thing to do because then the teacher can start to find his own solutions. He can always ask the advice of a colleague if he does not know what to do.

The problem is more serious if a parent complains. This may be in the form of a letter or at a parents' evening. Once again, it is not your place to take on the complaint and try to deal with it. The letter should be passed to the headteacher for him or her to decide what needs to be done. It is very rare for a parent to talk about one teacher to another, but if it does happen, intervene and ask them to make an appointment to discuss it with the teacher in person. Parents' evenings are reserved for discussing progress made by students. Time is often at a premium and cannot be wasted discussing the performance of your colleagues.

The room you booked is occupied

For weeks you have been planning a particular lesson and finally it has arrived. It is an opportunity to engage the class in a new concept that you find very interesting. You have put a great deal of time and effort into preparing the lesson, collecting the resources, and making sure the IT room is available. You lead your class to the room, and when you arrive you find, to your dismay, that it is already occupied. You check the booking and confirm you have reserved it. The other class have already logged on to the network and begun their lesson.

Your strategy

To widen access to expensive resources such as multi-gymnasiums, precision measuring equipment, the Internet etc. schools implement various booking systems. The staff who use them need to support the system and respect the rights of others who also use them.

When you find yourself in the position described above, go into the room and ask to speak to the teacher. Pick somewhere away from both sets of students and talk in a lowered voice so they cannot hear you. Explain that you had planned to use the room and booked it in advance. The other teacher may do one of two things. He may be extremely apologetic and say it was all his fault because he should have checked the booking form to make sure it was free, and offer you the room. Alternatively, he may dig in his heels and insist that he stays put because his students have already logged on and the lesson has started. Either way, the harm has been done, so there is little you can do about it now. By accepting his offer to move your problem is solved but he has got to get his class to log off, pack up and move out. You may decide it is easier to let him stay. This will give you the added inconvenience of postponing the lesson you have planned and having to think up something to do. Experienced teachers will usually have something ready for emergencies, so it is just a case of resorting to one of the pre-planned activities.

Avoid conflict

The best response is to back down unless you want to argue it out in front of the class. That will certainly not get you very far, and the students will revel in the experience of watching you both. It is far better to leave the room to him and then discuss it later.

When you meet with him, it is senseless arguing because you cannot turn the clock back. Point out that there is a booking system and you had reserved the room. You let him have it on that occasion but next time you will expect him to move for you. Then see the head of department in charge of the room and explain what happened and how you dealt with it. Ask her to remind everyone at the next staff meeting of the procedure for booking rooms to avoid this sort of thing happening again.

Equipment booking

Similar problems sometimes occur with items of equipment such as: video playback machines, televisions, and overhead projectors when they are used a lot and need to be booked. Last minute planning leads to rushing around gathering together equipment and resources. A television and video standing in the resources room may be a great temptation for the teacher panicking at the last minute. It may be booked and not collected, but that does not always mean it is free. The reservation book may not be handy, someone may have taken it to do their entries and not returned it so there is no way of checking who has booked what. The teacher who needs the equipment may feel they should have it rather than leave it unused. If you find the equipment you have booked has been taken by another teacher, what do you do?

If you have a fair idea of where the equipment has gone, you should go and check to see if it is there. The teacher may not have started using it so explain that you have booked it and need it for this lesson. He may claim that the reservation book was not around so he took the machine because he thought it was free. A mutually agreeable arrangement needs to be found. You could share it and have it for half of the lesson time each. He may stand firm and not want to part with it, so let him keep it, and talk it over later making sure you have the reservation book to show him your booking. Explain what happened to the technician in charge of the equipment and ask him or her to remind teachers at the next staff meeting of the procedure for booking equipment and the need to keep the reservation book in the room.

A colleague assisting in the classroom is contradicting you

For almost a term now you have enjoyed the help of a classroom assistant in one of your lessons. He has enabled you to try out a number of more complex activities and the whole class seems to be benefitting. However, just recently he seems to be contradicting things you are saying and sometimes getting the students to do things differently to the way you want them to. This needs addressing but you are aware that he is giving his services free and you do not know how to proceed.

Your strategy

Any extra help in the classroom is a bonus because it means that the students can receive more attention. This results in an improvement in both their behaviour and performance because the weaker students can keep up, and time can be given to stretch the more able. There are various types of classroom assistants available, including: parent helpers giving their time for free; paid assistants who will probably not have teaching qualifications; and learning support staff who will be qualified in giving specialist help to children with moderate to severe learning difficulties.

Parent helpers are usually more common in the pre-school and primary sector. They will offer their services for a few hours each week. They are of enormous value because they can listen to the children read regularly, which is something the teacher could not do unless he or she sidelined the rest of the curriculum.

Instructors and classroom assistants are usually part of the staff and receive payment for their services. They may not be qualified teachers and their function is to support – especially in subjects requiring specialist technical skills.

The learning support assistant is allocated to a class with students with specific learning difficulties. They are usually part of a learning support team in the institution. Their role during the lesson is to help the students with the work that the rest of the class is doing. Many teachers work with their assistants.

Learning support assistants also work to line managers who are responsible for co-ordinating the support for students on statements. Working with a number of people eventually leads to problems. The assistant is being directed by the teacher and may feel that he does not have enough autonomy. He may start to think he can do it better. Team-teaching relies on sharing ideas and working together for the good of the students. This requires time to plan, discuss and evaluate the activities and communication is the route to success. Without it, good practice and new ideas cannot be shared and allowed to flourish.

The problem in this scenario stems from not talking to each other. The classroom assistant (CA) is beginning to work against, rather than with the teacher. He may be a parent helper, giving his time willingly, so you need to be tactful when you talk to him.

Avoid conflict

Wait for a convenient moment after the lesson and then arrange to talk to him. Begin on a positive note by expressing your gratitude for her help.

T I just wanted to thank you for helping me. The children really like you, and it means I can spend more time with them individually.

CA Thank you. I am really enjoying it and they are great fun.

T I thought it would be useful if we spent some time discussing my ideas for the next English project.

The PE teacher has not asked if students can
be released from your lessons

You do not attempt to give criticism, instead you try to remedy the problem by involving the classroom assistant in the planning. It need not take long, just run the idea past him and get his views. Perhaps even let him look over the scheme of work and the possible resources for the project. Listen to him, he may have something useful to offer. Classroom assistants often see things differently to teachers because they are part of the 'audience'. When their suggestions seem like they could improve things, use them and do not feel threatened. They are not after your job but they do want to feel valued and able to help. A few words of praise goes a long way. People like to be told they are doing well and it does not take much effort to tell them.

This approach avoids any conflict and argument about what should be happening in the lesson. What has happened has gone and cannot be changed, resolve the problems by looking forward to better ways of working together.

The PE teacher has not asked if students can be released from your lessons

You are about to begin a lesson that will cover a particularly tricky topic when three students come and ask for permission to be released to play in a school football match. The PE teacher had not informed you of the match, or asked if your students could be excused. This is the second time it has happened since the start of the term.

Your strategy

When students want to do activities during lesson time such as trips out of school, rehearsals for plays, or sports, the same problem will occur and the burden will fall on you. School life is enriched by the range of activities on offer and students should be encouraged to take part in them. The consequences of missing lessons should be carefully explained to the students and they should be expected to make up the notes, do the homework that is set and see the teacher if they have any problems with the work before the next lesson. This will ensure that they do not fall behind and the teacher does not have to spend valuable lesson time helping individual students catch up.

There are several courses of action you can choose when students ask to be excused from your lesson and you have not been informed. The students may be trying it on, in which case you must decide whether to trust them or not. You could refuse on the grounds that you were not informed and therefore could not possibly let them go. They may feel resentful because they have a genuine reason for needing to be excused. To avoid this, send one of them to the PE teacher to ask for a note releasing them. Once you have the note you can let them go.

Reminding about procedures

Raise the matter of requesting the release of students from lessons with the teacher concerned. Point out that this is not the first time it has happened. Remind them of the school procedure which may be a note on the staff noticeboard or a mention at the staff briefing at the start of the week. Finish by stating that you are prepared to let students leave your lesson for good reasons, but only if you are given prior warning. There will be a condition attached to agreeing to release them, the students must make up missed work in their own time so they do not fall behind. You may feel that talking directly to your colleague places you in an awkward position, in which case you should talk to the head of department and explain the problem. They can follow it up and make sure the correct procedure is followed in future.

Another teacher regularly detains your class

One of your groups of students always turns up late for the lesson. They have to walk from the other end of the school to reach your room. There is no changeover time between the lessons, so collaboration between teachers is essential. The teacher who takes them before you is notorious for over-running and packing up late. He has been at the school for nearly twenty years and does not take kindly to younger colleagues and their requests.

Your strategy

There is always one like him! He is a law unto himself and has become quite powerful to the point that the other staff prefer to leave him be than try to change things. They feel intimidated by him and he knows it.

The late arrival of the students is resulting in the loss of between five and ten minutes of a forty-five minute lesson every week. Clearly this cannot continue because it will be very hard to cover the syllabus in the year. Ask one or two of the more responsible students why they keep arriving late. Once you have established that the delay is definitely due to leaving the previous lesson after the bell you can decide what to do about it. Talking to the teacher does not seem to be an easy option but you should try to first of all. Arrange to meet him when he is not busy and has the time to listen to you. Explain your situation and politely ask him to let the class go promptly on the bell. At this point he may try to justify their lateness with explanations about how much work he has to cover in too short a time, and the time taken to clear up equipment. Resist getting drawn into a discussion. He has a responsibility to let the students get to the next lesson on time by dismissing them punctually. By all means listen to him and sympathise if you have the time, but conclude by reiterating your request:

> 'Well, I would appreciate it if you can let them out promptly when the bell goes.'

Then wait and see what happens next lesson. If the class arrives late you will need to try something else.

Taking the matter further

The usual thing is to talk over the problem with your head of department or line manager. Explain the situation and what you have done to try to resolve it. Your head of department can then talk to the other teacher's head of department who will then try to find a solution for the problem. She may offer some suggestions for improving the delivery of the curriculum and managing the time. She will make clear the need to respect the time of other teachers. After all, you may be experiencing the same problems as him so you are entitled to your full lesson time as much as anyone. The problem may continue so you should be prepared to go back and repeat your request to your head of department and expect some action.

Bad breath

> Lunchtime duty enables you to get to know some of your students in a more informal setting. You usually try to move around, pausing to have a brief chat with various groups about their games or things they are interested in. On one occasion you stop to talk to several boys about their collection of stickers. You lean forward to comment on a particular page and one of the boys stands back and exclaims:
>
> 'Aw Sir, your breath smells evil!'
>
> You cannot help showing your embarrassment.

Your strategy

Teachers are expected to be clean and dress smartly to set the students an example to follow, and to reinforce the system they are part of. Personal hygiene is very important when you are working with people. Bad breath or halitosis is a condition that can be avoided but we are not always aware of it. Regular cleaning of teeth and gums will keep it at bay. However, a particularly piquant evening meal cooked in garlic, or perhaps an Indian take-away will leave its mark. Be prepared, by using a breath freshener in the morning and at lunchtime to keep the 'wolf' at bay.

Even after taking care you may still find yourself in the situation described above and need a way out of it. A simple apology may suffice:

> 'I'm sorry (standing back a bit). Have you got the whole set of stickers yet?'

Try humour.

You could say something funny like:

> 'I'm sorry, I must speak to cook about what she is putting in those dinners.'
>
> 'I'm sorry, I was taking part in the international curry eating championship last night.'
>
> 'I'm sorry, I have been trying out the new garlic toothpaste for a well-known toothpaste manufacturer ... it's not very good is it?'
>
> 'Yes sorry, don't stand too close. I use it on children who have been naughty and I forgot to switch it off.'
>
> 'Sorry, I was in a play last night as an evil dragon and I had to use the fire breath drops to make it realistic.'

Finding humour in a difficult situation helps to lighten it, and shows you have the capacity to make fun of yourself. It gives you the opportunity of getting away behind a smokescreen of laughter and if they like the joke it will help you feel a bit better after such a harsh personal criticism has just been levelled at you.

Students give you a nickname

During break you notice some of your students looking in your direction and sniggering. After a while you realise that they have given you a nickname. Normally it would not bother you but the name is a particularly hurtful one that draws attention to a part of your body that is far from perfect. Several weeks go by but you are still feeling embarrassed and hurt by it and you resent the nickname. You feel that if it continues it will make you dislike the students and prejudice your judgement of their work.

Your strategy

You need a solution that will not make you an even bigger object of ridicule. Nicknames are bestowed on people for many reasons and once it starts, it becomes a tradition to give every teacher one. The most common method of naming is based on visual features. I once knew a teacher who became known as 'Arnie' because he was slightly built and was the complete opposite of Arnold Schwarzenegger, the Hollywood actor with the well-developed physique. Then there was my science teacher, a formidable man over six foot tall. He became fondly known by everyone as 'Big Jim', although how he got the name 'Jim' escapes me. Teachers get given derogatory nicknames usually because they are unpopular for whatever reason.

Once a name is given it often sticks for many years and becomes absorbed into the popular mythology of the school. You cannot force the students to stop calling you it, but you can deter them from doing it publicly so the effects are minimised. Eventually they may get tired of using it because they cannot call you it openly without risk of punishment if they are heard.

You may already be aware of a name students have given you and it does not worry you. You may even use it to improve your relationship with the class. The difficulty arises when you do not feel comfortable with a nickname. There is a way of dealing with it but it takes time and effort. Take some time out from the usual programme to talk to the class about respect. There is a lot of material available as it is a topic usually covered in the PSE programmes in schools.

Begin by helping your students to understand what you mean by respect, and then get them to try and empathise with being disabled, bullied, or of a different ethnic origin or religion. Prejudice often begins with name-calling and so it is an ideal issue to tackle through role-play. You should bring in the subject of nicknames at this point and follow it up by talking about how it feels when the recipient of a nickname takes it seriously and is hurt by it. (You do not tell them that you personally find it hurtful. Give the impression that you are ignoring it.)

Spending time in this way is a valuable investment because it will help your own group of students become more sensitive to the feelings of other people. It may eventually solve the problem of your own nickname. When you hear students calling you or anyone by a nickname in the future you can refer them back to your lesson and how they felt when they role-played the victim.

Involve others

You may not feel confident to give the lesson on your own so seek advice and guidance from drama teachers or colleagues who deliver PSE programmes. They are used to dealing with this kind of issue and often employ role-play and empathy acting in their lessons. When you have done it once it will no longer seem a daunting task.

The school disco and student 'crushes' on teachers

> The lights are flashing and the music is pounding as the upper school disco nears to a close. It has been a very successful event and everyone appears to have thoroughly enjoyed themselves. Suddenly the beat of the music changes, the lights stop flashing and the hall is thrown into a subdued darkness, signalling that it is time for the last slow dance. The subtle, fluid movement of the liquid oil wheel projects globular images on the walls and bathes the couples dancing together with warm light. As you look on, one of the older students comes and asks you to dance.

Your strategy

How can you refuse? To say no would appear cruel in her eyes and the rejection would shatter her ego, not to mention her image in the eyes of her friends who are watching and waiting to see what your reaction will be. But 'no' is what you must say. You cannot say yes because it will place you in a position that could compromise your professional integrity as a teacher. The girl has asked you to dance to a slow record with her which requires the partners to be face to face, with their bodies close. No matter how innocent you may think the request is, others may not read it that way. They will see a teacher, arm in arm with a young student in a darkened room dancing in a way normally associated with courting couples. This threatens the conventions of the teacher-student relationship based on giving professional help.

Be firm

Try and say no in a way that will not offend the student. There are ways this can be done and it is down to individual choice how you do it. Some replies could be:

> 'I am flattered that you have asked me but I shall have to say no.'
> 'I appreciate your offer, but I have to go and supervise the cloak-room in a minute.'

These replies begin with a compliment and then decline the request. You do not have to give a reason, simply saying no should suffice, but if you feel you need to, say that you will have to go and do something like supervise the cloakroom, car park, or refreshments. Be warned she may persist if it is early in the evening so you will need several reasons ready to use. Try not to lead her on with excuses like:

> 'If I was ten years younger I would love to but I am afraid I have got to say no.'

She will not be satisfied with this because the age difference does not enter into it. Also avoid weak excuses such as:

> 'I can't dance.'
> 'I am too old.'
> 'You don't want to dance with me when there are all these good-looking boys waiting for the chance.'

She does, that is why she asked you! She will teach you to dance and argue that you are not too old. She will tell you that older men are more attractive and younger boys do not appeal to her. Of course, if you are already married or in a relationship you can tell the truth.

> 'I am flattered, but my wife will not approve.'
> 'I never dance with anyone except my wife.'

Telling students you are married or in a steady relationship is the most effective way of dealing with student crushes, but you do need to keep the story going with the occasional 'press releases' about your partner. Some students will ignore every excuse you give them and persist. When a student will not accept no for an answer in the kind of situation described you must be direct and honest:

> 'Teachers do not dance with their students because other people would get the wrong idea. So I must say no.'

It is very important for teachers to keep their distance and remain professional in these situations.

Avoid being overfamiliar

There is a temptation to encourage students who have a crush on you by being overly friendly to them. They are at a very impressionable age and look to you for the right ways of behaving. Teachers need to be aware of their position and make sure they do not do anything to lead their students on.

The messages we give should be clear and unambiguous. Overfamiliarity can be misunderstood by those students who already feel attracted to a teacher. Make sure you are careful in what you say if you find yourself in this position. Balance politeness and friendliness with professional distance to avoid being too familiar or acting coldly.

Involve others

Finally, always alert a colleague or your line manager if you think a student has a crush on you and seek their help if you think you need it. Put on record your concern if it starts to look tricky. Then take special care not to place yourself in a compromising position that could lead to difficulties, such as being alone with the student. (See also 'Alone in a room with a student of the opposite sex', p. 137.)

Kissing under the mistletoe

Christmas has come around again and it is the last week of term. Quite a few of the upper school students and sixth formers have brought in sprigs of mistletoe and are making merry in the traditional way. During the morning break you meet a group of particularly exuberant youngsters and one of them approaches you brandishing a festive branch and looking intent on getting a kiss beneath it, as is the custom.

Your strategy

Duck into the nearby office and escape! Christmas is a time of peace and goodwill, but making merry in this way is a dangerous occupation for teachers. The innocent 'peck' under the mistletoe can lead to all sorts of problems. Teachers like to be friendly with their students but the line needs to be drawn somewhere to preserve their status. Kissing students, even under mistletoe can put doubts into some people's minds about a teacher.

The moment you realise they are coming for you, hold up your hand with your palm facing them in the way a police officer stops traffic. This will signal to them that you want them to stop where they are immediately. It will also create a barrier between you and them. Once they have stopped you can speak:

T   Just a minute please, girls.

This indicates to them that you want their attention and places them on the alert. Ask them a question about anything or go straight to the point:

T   I can see you are getting in the festive mood but I am going to have to ask you to go outside now because this corridor should be kept clear.

Then move to the main issue by addressing the girl who was coming for you.

T   Kissing may be an enjoyable Christmas tradition but please confine it to boys of your own age, you may scare the others!

The last comment cleverly conceals any reference to you or a specific age group, older or younger. Alternatively, you could ask them to put the mistletoe away until after school.

T   You may enjoy kissing under the mistletoe, but it is inappropriate behaviour while in school. So either give it to me to look after or put it in your bag until you go home please.

The girls can then choose what they want to do without feeling they are being controlled.

Alone in a room with a student of the opposite sex

The photography club is very popular as an after-school activity. One afternoon, the teacher is working in the darkroom with four students on a printing job. Three of them decide to go out and begin packing up, leaving the teacher in the room with a student of the opposite sex.

Your strategy

It is foolish to take unnecessary risks. Just think what *might* happen. The girl has been harbouring a grudge against the teacher for some time and has hatched a plan. She joined the photography club recently and seemed very keen. The teacher enjoyed her enthusiasm and was very relaxed when she was around. One day her chance arrived, the others left the room and she found herself alone with him. The room was dimly lit by one red bulb.

She turns away from the sink where they had been developing some prints together and went to the other end of the room where the film dryer stood. There was nothing unusual about that. Students would often check the progress of films. The teacher was oblivious of what she was doing in the dimly lit, far corner of the room. He carried on working. She turned her back on him and began undoing the buttons of her shirt. She pulled her tie down and dishevelled her hair. Then glancing over her shoulder to check what he was doing she suddenly let out a piercing scream and shouted:

'No ... stop, get away from me!'

and fled the room with tears streaming down her face.

This is simply an example of what *could* happen if a teacher had been left alone with a student of the opposite sex. The teacher did not do anything but he would find it very hard to prove his innocence. Even if he could prove he had not done anything, his reputation would be tarnished and a question mark would hang over him from that day on.

Avoid the problem

The rule is simple. Never be in a closed room without windows with a small number of students of the opposite sex. Your professional reputation and livelihood are at stake so you cannot take the risk no matter how much you think you can trust the students.

Try to keep at least four people in the room with you. The moment the numbers drop to below an acceptable level, leave and tell the students where you will be. They can bring their work out to you when they need to. Then remain outside until everyone has finished and left the room, or until you need to demonstrate something to a larger group. Some students will hang around at the end and you may need to clean up and turn things off. To get them out you should send in a student rather than go in yourself.

A similar situation

This might occur with games, swimming and PE, so you should be aware of the potential 'danger'. It goes without saying that you do not enter the changing rooms of the opposite sex in a secondary school. Send a student in if you want them to hurry or you need someone from the class. In primary schools the arrangements for changing may be different. The children may get changed in the classrooms and usually it only involves getting in and out of their PE kit. Swimming involves removing all of their clothing so it would not be wise to venture into the changing rooms at all if you are male, or unless it is really necessary if you are female. Appointing a responsible child as a monitor to make sure the room is cleared and left tidy is one solution. Children begin to develop an awareness of their bodies at an early age so it is right that you respect their privacy whenever possible. You can stand at the door and monitor them while they are changing without having to go right in.

Summary

Knowing what to ignore and what to follow up is a skill that only really comes with experience. The skill is in remaining silent when you know your comments will not change things. Waiting for tempers to calm down before responding is crucial. There is seldom anything to gain from rushing into an argument with a colleague while one or both of you are still fired up and angry. Leave it for a day or two so you can think more clearly about what you are going to do and say.

Managing colleagues is more of a challenge than managing students and their behaviour. The most common form of management is 'top-down' with managers managing the rest of the staff. Some of the examples in this chapter offer ways of reversing this model and preventing problems occurring by pre-empting them.

Preserving the integrity of the profession is the responsibility of everyone involved. This begins by acknowledging that there are agreed codes of behaviour. Only then can we begin to support each other and ensure that our students receive the best we can provide.

Key points for fostering good working relationships with colleagues and students

- Never comment or discuss a member of staff in front of the students.
- Insist that discussions about your own performance as a teacher take place in private, and remain confidential.
- When another class is disturbing yours try to talk it over with their teacher in a helpful, non-aggressive way.
- Do not allow students to discuss other staff with you. Stop them and tell them it would be unprofessional of you to listen.
- When a colleague double-books resources you have already reserved, let him have them if he have started using them but point out that next time you will expect him to give them up to you. Inform your head of department and ask them to remind everyone of the procedure for reservations.
- Keep classroom assistants informed and involve them in your planning.
- Insist that teachers who want your students released from lessons for extra-curricular activities notify you in advance.
- Expect other teachers to respect your lesson time and get the students to you punctually.
- Maintain your appearance and personal hygiene.
- Deal with nicknames as part of a PSE activity about prejudice. Use role-play and empathy to help students understand how it feels to be a victim.

Summary

- Keep your distance with students of the opposite sex, especially at Christmas and at informal social events.
- Never let yourself get into a situation when you are alone in a room with a student of the opposite sex.

An individual approach to managing behaviour

The following list contains some suggested 'dos' and 'don'ts' to support your individual management of students' behaviour.

Do not

- Give a detention that you cannot supervise. Other teachers should not have to deal with your misbehavers.
- Give whole class punishments for something only a few students were responsible for.
- Give punishments that are out of proportion to the misdemeanour.
- Give after-school detentions without prior notice. Most schools have a procedure for notifying parents.
- Physically touch students e.g. grabbing, slapping, pushing.
- Send a student out of the class without arranging for their supervision.
- Punish a student without being certain of their action.
- Deal with a student while you are angry.

Do

- Give students choices so they can own their behaviour.
- Ignore attention-seeking behaviour when it is undesirable.
- Allow students to fix the situation.
- Raise your voice when someone is behaving in a dangerous way. Immediately the situation is under control return to your normal way of speaking.
- Allow take-up time for students to respond.
- Be certain. If in doubt, find out more before you act.

- Make the consequences of an action clear.
- Allow a student to rebuild damaged relationships after breaking a rule.
- Link the consequence to the fault, e.g. littering can be dealt with by tidying up.
- End the punishment when it is carried out. Do not bear grudges.

Towards a whole school approach

Here are some key points that you may like to consider when developing a policy for the management of behaviour in your school.

Aims

- Involve everyone: teachers, support staff, administrative staff, site supervisors, cleaners, canteen staff etc.
- Develop a plan that incorporates the views of students, staff, governors and parents.
- Give students greater responsibility in managing their own behaviour.

How to do it

- Get everyone talking about behaviour management. Make it a regular agenda item at meetings e.g. ask staff to talk about an 'incident', and get the group to consider strategies. Record these incidents and the solutions.
- Set aside INSET time to look at the most common problems. Bring in a consultant to help by taking an objective view of how you are coping.
- Shift solutions from a controlling discipline administered by teachers to student centred approaches.
- Inform parents of your policy.
- Produce a manual of 'incidents' for use by all staff.
- Get teachers to produce behaviour plans for their difficult groups.

- Train all new, and newly-qualified staff, in the methods advocated by your school.
- Observe each other so that skills in behaviour management can be shared.
- Review the effects of your policy regularly.

Some helpful books

This brief list is not a full bibliography, but a very selective small collection of books especially helpful to all teachers and managers.

Laslett, R., and Smith, C.J., *Effective Classroom Management*, Routledge, 1993.

Lund, R., A *Whole-School Behaviour Policy*, Kogan Page, 1996.

Marland, M., *The Craft of the Classroom*, Heinemann Educational, 1993.

Montgomery, D., *Managing Behaviour Problems*, Hodder and Stoughton, 1989.

Robertson, J., *Effective Classroom Control*, Hodder and Stoughton, 1996.

Rogers, B., *Behaviour Recovery. A Programme for Behaviourally Disordered Students in Mainstream Schools*, ACER, 1994.

Willis, P., *Learning to Labour*, Arena, 1993.